# A HISTORY OF MOUNT SAINT CHARLES HOCKEY

**BRYAN ETHIER**

*Foreword by* ASSISTANT COACH PAUL GUAY

Published by The History Press
Charleston, SC 29403
www.historypress.net

Copyright © 2013 by Bryan Ethier
All rights reserved

*Front cover, top*: Courtesy of Ernest Brown.
*Front cover, bottom*: Courtesy of Ernest Brown.
*Back cover, top right*: Courtesy of Ernest Brown.

First published 2013

Manufactured in the United States

ISBN 978.1.60949.879.5

Library of Congress CIP data applied for.

Notice: The information in this book is true and complete to the best of our knowledge. It is offered without guarantee on the part of the author or The History Press. The author and The History Press disclaim all liability in connection with the use of this book.

All rights reserved. No part of this book may be reproduced or transmitted in any form whatsoever without prior written permission from the publisher except in the case of brief quotations embodied in critical articles and reviews.

*To my wife, Debbie, my daughters, Jordan and Brooke, and my son, Adam, for condoning my road trips to Adelard Arena and my funky moods on those rare occasions when Mount loses.*

# CONTENTS

Foreword, by Paul Guay     7
Acknowledgements     9

PART I: THE BIRTH AND EVOLUTION OF MOUNT SAINT CHARLES HOCKEY
1. The Circle of Life     13
2. The Brother Adelard Era     19

PART II: THE RESURRECTION OF MOUNT PRIDE: THE LARRY KISH ERA
3. How the Flying Frenchmen Became the Foundering Frenchmen     27
4. The Creation of Mount Pride     30
5. Skating Through Russia to Get to Woonsocket     47

PART III: ASCENSION INTO GREATNESS
6. The "House" That Coach Bill Built     57
7. Streaking Through the Streak: Highlights of the Twenty-six Consecutive Mount Saint Charles State Championships     68

PART IV: GREAT GAMES, GREAT SERIES, GREAT MOMENTS
8. "The First": The Streak Begins with the 1978 State Championship     85
9. The Fourteen-Second Miracle     87
10. Hawks Snowed Under     91
11. Nothing Lasts Forever: King Titans End the Streak     95

## Contents

PART V: ANATOMY OF A RIVALRY ... 99

PART VI: THE CULTURE OF MOUNT SAINT CHARLES HOCKEY
12. John Guevremont, Class of 1976: Spreading the Word(s) ... 109
13. Richard Lawrence, MSC Director of Athletics: Keeping Sports in Perspective ... 115
14. Ed Lee: From Street Punk to Student Healer ... 119
15. It's a Family Affair: The Influence of Mount Hockey on John, Bill, Dave and Peter Belisle ... 127

Bibliography ... 139
Index ... 141
About the Author ... 143

# FOREWORD

I suppose there are many images of the Mount Saint Charles Hockey program—each person with his or her own take on how it came to have all of the success it has had. I had my own glorious image of the Flying Frenchmen from when I was a small boy and my father would take me to almost every game. The team would come racing on to the ice as the cheerleaders sang "When the Saints Go Marching In." Some of the players had red-white-and-blue skates, which was mesmerizing for a small boy, as no one else wore colored skates. And they were good—good. I thought, "Maybe one day I might be able to play for the Mount!"

When I entered the ninth grade, Mount had a very strong program led by a coach I had had in Squirt hockey, Mr. Belisle. The team had barely lost in the state championship the previous year, and I was hopeful to make the team and be a part of the glorious tradition. The rose-colored glasses I had on the first day of practice quickly turned clear, as I realized there was a huge jump from youth hockey to high school hockey. And the work ethic and commitment had to be ratcheted up a bit—but only like a thousand times. Although I thought I was a good player, I was clearly now in the deep end of the pool!

We had a great team, and the coach had huge expectations of all the players. To do a drill meant doing it perfectly. Skating drills were to be done at full speed *all* of the time. Not skating hard was letting your teammates down, so we would continue skating until 100 percent of the players were giving 100 percent. You may have been a big fish before, but now even the big fish were little fish. And the coach couldn't have cared less for your thoughts on how the Mount would play or who would play. He was pushing all of the players to be the best they could be and to play the game as a team—no individuals need apply. Coach was teaching us to expect more from ourselves and to try to improve every day. The deficiencies we had were pointed out, but we were also learning to recognize and correct flaws in our own game. Coach was always objective and honest with all of us in regard to our play, and we were doing our own self-assessment in order to be the best that we could be. Mount hockey molded players that were coveted by college coaches and even some pro scouts. Why? Because the players understood how to play the game the right way—as a team and with 100 percent commitment to the success of the team. And the work ethic was without question.

As players are going through the program and learning what is expected of them at Mount in order to be successful, they are being taught life lessons about what it will take to be successful in life as well as the importance of commitment, hard work and being honest with yourself and trying to improve upon your weaknesses. We are not always going to be big fish, and not every day is going to be a victory, but by doing things the right way every day, your successes will outnumber the defeats. We didn't realize it at the time, but it certainly is clear as an adult. Life lessons learned through a game that we all love and from a coach who always knew what he was teaching was much larger than the game itself.

PAUL GUAY
*Mount Saint Charles Class of 1981*

# ACKNOWLEDGEMENTS

I would like to thank the following for their input and assistance in making this project viable:

Ernest Brown, for his many cover-worthy photos; the Belisle family, for their honesty and direction; Tony Ciresi, for his sense of humor and his kick saves in 1972; Larry Kish, for the creation of the Mount hockey "blur"; Ed Lee, for reminding us that we are all teachers and healers; Gail Bryson, for her connections, photos and guidance; the Brothers of the Sacred Heart, for the Spirit that continues to flow through Mount Saint Charles Academy and its students, coaches, teachers, staff and alumni; the scores of blessed young men who have donned the Mount colors for some ninety seasons; and the many others who gave their time, voices and memories of hockey life on Logee Street.

Part I

# THE BIRTH AND EVOLUTION OF MOUNT SAINT CHARLES HOCKEY

## Chapter 1
# THE CIRCLE OF LIFE

Brendan Belisle never led his Mount Saint Charles (MSC) hockey team in scoring. Yet the assist he recorded on June 12, 2013, ranks as one of the most historic in the program's vaunted history. On a sunny and cheerful day when many twenty-one-year-olds would have been outside being, well, twenty-one, Belisle and two other co-workers teamed to install protective Plexiglas, pane by pane, atop the dasher boards at a semi-dark and shadowy Mount Saint Charles Arena. One of the many improvements that will vault the beloved yet archaic hockey cathedral into the modern era, the standard faux glass replaces the antiquated trademark chain-link fence that, for fifty seasons, helped to create much of the character that has made this arena so unique.

For Mount hockey aficionados, as each link of metal fence went to the wayside, with it went a historic and poignant link to a special Mount player, championship and moment. In this arena, Coach Larry Kish resurrected a floundering Mount program, leading the Mount to the 1967–68 state title, its first in twenty seasons, as well as the 1972 championship. Here, Mount began its historic streak of twenty-six straight Rhode Island titles, including ten straight national titles. In this arena, Bill Belisle became the most successful high school hockey coach in the country, two Mount players vaulted to the top spot in the NHL draft and dozens of others skated their way onto college hockey programs. Alas, time waits for no one, not even MSC and this erstwhile aircraft hangar it has called home since 1963.

It should come as no surprise that a member of the Belisle clan was helping to improve the tired building. When you are of Belisle pedigree, you help others before you help yourself. Bill Belisle learned that lesson as a kid growing up in Manville, Rhode Island, and he has spent a lifetime and innumerable Mount practices imparting that sense of selflessness to his biological family and to his hockey players. As son Dave once said, the arena is "my father's house."

Belisle's most personalized room, doubtless, is his office, a pictorial shrine to the hockey program and its accomplishments. Like the soon-to-be-erstwhile chain-link fence, this pseudo-museum is a link to great players, great moments, great teams and great championships. Virtually every inch of wall space in this closet-sized "man cave" is consumed by photographs of Mount players—from Paul Guay to Brian Lawton to Garth Snow to Bryan Berard to Dave Belisle—state commendations trumpeting the program's

Following his team's 2013 state championship victory, Dave Belisle honors his father with a respectful kiss on the forehead. *Photo Courtesy of Ernest Brown.*

accomplishments or newspaper clippings chronicling another state title during "The Streak." It's hard to miss the oversized hand-drawn "We Miss You, Mr. Belisle" get-well card signed by each of the Mount students after Belisle's near-fatal fall during the 1982–83 season. A hockey stick donated by former Mount and NHL all-star Mathieu Schneider stands in one corner of the room. To the uninitiated, all of this Mount "stuff" may appear to be little more than callous self-promotion. Bill Belisle, however, has never required external validation. The room, he'll tell you, honors his kids.

If memorabilia and artifacts clutter the floor and walls of this hockey room, the desk of Arena Manager Belisle is a picture of order: a white desktop computer sits neatly to the left, a large calculator to the right and a large business calendar in between. Most curious, however, is the container that holds about a dozen pencils. Each No. 2 graphite is sharpened to a deadly point, and each stands on its eraser, poised and peering skyward like a Mount player ready to take the ice. If you have ever wondered if Bill Belisle's demand for perfection, order and precision extends only to his hockey players, especially during the practices he runs, you need only consider those sharpened pencils.

These two stories that connect three generations of Belisles serve as poignant reminders of how difficult it can be for the Mount community to relinquish the glorious past, when Rhode Island high school hockey is in such a state of flux. For instance, in many ways, the 2012–13 Mount hockey team was the most remarkable under the Belisle regime. Although Mount swept LaSalle Academy in two games to win the state title, the program's forty-third overall, little came easy in '13. All-state forward Brian Belisle (Brendan's younger brother and Dave's son) was sidelined until early February with a concussion, suffered in the season opener against Cranston West. Two other Mount forwards lost valuable playing time also because of concussions. Unlike its predecessors, the 2013 club lacked the depth to compensate for the loss of three starters, especially the dynamic Brian Belisle. As a result, for the first time in his coaching career, Bill Belisle lacked the depth to call up a single player from a JV team that finished 5–6–1. The initial ramifications of such attrition were, by Mount standards, ungodly. Without Brian Belisle in the lineup, Mount scrambled to get out of the Cimini Division basement; included in the rough start was a shocking January 19 shutout loss to Coventry High, the defending Division II champion.

Yet what could have been an ugly season slowly evolved into another typical Mount finish. The Mount coaching staff stuck with its system and showed the unseasoned players how to apply the Mount Style. In early February

2013, doctors okayed Brian Belisle to play. With the team captain back in the fold and his teammates evolving into a cohesive unit, Mount dispatched LaSalle in the finals with relative ease. Ironically, Bishop Hendricken, the defending state champ and regular-season division winner in 2012–13, lost in the opening round of the playoffs to LaSalle. So how did Mount go from division pretenders to winners and Hendricken from winners to non-contenders so quickly?

For years, many of the state's best hockey players have left Rhode Island high school hockey programs to ply their trade for prep schools or junior programs. That's no secret. Over the last dozen years, however, not only have gilt-edged players left early, but so have numerous players yet to make their mark on their local teams. Why the pipeline out of the RIIL? Today's hockey player—star and role player, both—is tempted by more hockey and academic options than ever before, from the dozens of New England prep schools to the scores of junior hockey programs. The result? The talent is more diluted than ever, not just in the RIIL but also in the prep ranks. The Belisles, however, sympathize. If a prep school waves thousands of dollars in scholarship money in a player's face, who in today's tight economy can resist? According to Dave Belisle:

> *When kids call up and say they want to leave, we don't say, "Don't leave, don't leave." They have to do what's best for their family. Every decision is different, and you have to go with your mother and father. We're not going to get in your way because, in your heart, you've already made that decision. If you have the opportunity to go for free and you don't have to whip out $12,000 a year the way bills are coming, you know what? I'm sorry—I have to do it. We understand. It hurts, but we understand. Financially, it's just a wiser decision. We've come to handle it pretty well; we don't take it to heart. Ten, fifteen years ago, it was really killing us. Now it's like, "Who's next?"*

With so many new faces appearing at tryouts, it has become a challenge for coaches to maintain a sense of tradition and momentum in their programs. That scenario played a role in Moses Brown's decision to pull the hockey program from the Rhode Island Interscholastic League (RIIL) after the 2011–12 season. Dave Belisle says he has discussed with other area coaches the potential for an all–Catholic schools league or another independent league that would feature traditionally powerful hockey programs. Still, the idea of stalwarts MSC, Hendricken and LaSalle breaking ranks to play a

# THE BIRTH AND EVOLUTION OF MOUNT SAINT CHARLES HOCKEY

The Mount Saint Charles coaching staff prides itself in scheduling games against some of the best clubs in America. One of its stiffest opponents was Academy of Holy Angels of South Richfield, Minnesota. Here, the two teams pose for a group photograph after squaring off in Minnesota. *Photo courtesy of Bill Belisle.*

MSC players pile onto each other in celebration of one of the team's forty-three Rhode Island state titles. *Photo courtesy of Bill Belisle.*

schedule packed exclusively with prep powers such as Deerfield Academy, Avon Old Farms or Belmont Hill is difficult to envision.

So Bill and Dave Belisle and assistants Paul Guay and Peter Capizzo do what they do best: they teach the kids who want to play hockey for Mount Saint Charles. For instance, on June 12, 2113, some six months before the start of the 2013–14 campaign, Mount already had lost Tyler Scroggins, its top returning forward, to a prep school. Others may follow. Still, Mount expects to return in 2013–14 all-star senior goalie Brian Larence, bullish defenseman Keith Phaneuf and quick and talented forward Patrick Holmes.

The thought of entering a new season with a core of just three players would make most coaches write their letters of resignation. Dave and Bill Belisle, however, chuckle ironically. They'll find a way to win. After all, despite the many changes in the landscape of Rhode Island high school hockey, MSC still boasts the Mount Style, Mount Pride and two coaches named Belisle.

## Chapter 2
# THE BROTHER ADELARD ERA

Twenty-six.

Given the diluted state of Rhode Island high school hockey, it's hard to imagine how Mount Saint Charles managed to reel off twenty-six straight Rhode Island high school state championships between 1978 and 2003. Richard Lawrence, Mount's director of athletics, witnessed each of them. "I have asked myself that question a lot of times," says Lawrence. "There are other schools that have their own rink and knowledgeable people; how do you win twenty-six state championships in a row? How does that happen? Success breeds success. Still, that doesn't answer the question of twenty-six state titles in a row."

Many times during his coaching career, Bill Belisle attributed the success to the mystical force called "Mount Pride." Meanwhile, opposing teams and their fans lamented that "Mount always gets the best players," although that was not always the case. Some pointed to Mount's wellspring of practice time, conducted in its fickle, diminutive backyard hockey rink. Many attribute the success to the coaching staff, for years led by the father-son duo of Bill and Dave Belisle, augmented by a handful of excellent assistants. Each of these factors contributed to Mount's unparalleled success for twenty-six seasons.

"Contributed" is the operative word. MSC is much more than just wins and losses and state and national hockey titles; Mount Saint Charles Academy is a culture in and of itself. In that culture, you will find the true source for the creation and life of The Streak.

The birth of Mount hockey is woven in equal parts spirit and, well, yarn. In the mid-1850s, the area now known as the Woonsocket comprised six thriving mill villages: Woonsocket Falls Village, Bernon Mills Village, Social Village, Jenkesville, Hamlet Village and Globe Village. Nestled around the Blackstone River, these mill villages comprised communities of workers who toiled in the massive red-bricked, wood or stone textile-producing mills. As the local textile industry expanded, so did the need for additional manpower, and legions of workers were pipelined from Quebec to fill the ranks. Such recruiting of French Canadians lasted for nearly a century, eventually depleting Quebec of nearly one-third of its population and, in turn, transforming New England into a hub for the manufacturing of textiles. By 1888, the year Woonsocket was formed from the six mill villages, a tight-knit city built upon a solid foundation of brick and mortar, hard work and solid religious faith had been established. In 1900, 60 percent of the townspeople were of French Canadian descent, and the city of Woonsocket had earned the honor as the most "French city in the country."

After World War II, textile manufacturing faded out in Woonsocket. The abandoned brick, stone and wood buildings stood as silent, lifeless monuments to a once-thriving industry and a once-thriving town. With multi-family tenement buildings huddled around the idle mills and somber, pious churches stationed around town, Woonsocket for many years thereafter resembled a city stuck in time, unable to establish a new business paradigm and cultural persona.

Despite the change in the Woonsocket business landscape, many of the descendants of the original French Canadian mill workers began to fill the ranks of the Mount Saint Charles hockey teams, as would other "imports" from Quebec. A new spirit swept into Woonsocket—to Logee Street, to be specific. Seeing a need to instruct the residents of Woonsocket (especially the children of the Canadian immigrants), to keep alive the language and to spark the Catholic faith, Monsignor Charles Dauray, pastor of Precious Blood Parish, invited the Brothers of the Sacred Heart to staff a local school. In 1919, Mount Saint Charles Academy was incorporated, and five years later, the school opened its doors to both boarders and commuters. By accepting boarders, the school unwittingly opened the door, literally, to Canadian hockey players who fostered a Mount–Montreal Canadiens connection that, to this day, still exists.

In the 1930s, ownership of the school was transferred to the Brothers of the Sacred Heart, who staffed the academy with Brothers from New England. A standard of academics, spirituality and respect was established and remains the foundation upon which students learn, profess their faith and, yes, play hockey.

# The Birth and Evolution of Mount Saint Charles Hockey

If the Brothers of the Sacred Heart brought a spiritual essence to the academic community, a simple man brought a passion for both the Lord and shots on goal. A native of Saint Jean Deschaillons, Quebec, Brother Adelard Beaudet grew up skating on the nearby frozen Saint Lawrence River. At age twenty, Adelard took his religious vows and in 1911 was sent to Sacred Heart Academy in Central Falls to spread the Word. And as he did, Brother Adelard began to spread the gospel of hockey.

When he began coaching at Sacred Heart Academy in Central Falls, hockey was played on frozen ponds, and scant equipment consisted of tree branches flattened into rudimentary sticks and pads (when used) created from mail-in catalogs or schoolbooks bound to fragile ankles. Both rubber pucks and balls were used, and players' jackets were anchored on the ice by rocks and used as goal nets. Rules were few, and games went sixty minutes—without line changes or timeouts or breaks to resurface the ice (which was then impossible).

The "Founding Father of Rhode Island Hockey," Brother Adelard Beaudet, launched the Mount Saint Charles hockey program in the mid-1920s. Between 1933 and 1947, Adelard's Mounties won ten state titles. *Photo courtesy of Mount Saint Charles.*

When Mount Saint Charles Academy opened in 1924, Brother Adelard was there to greet students and to promote his beloved sport. High school hockey's beginnings were equally modest, with a four-team league composed of Mount, LaSalle Academy, Classical High and Central High of Providence competing, for the most part, on an outdoor ice rink constructed by Adelard and a few other hockey enthusiasts. Four years later, the Rhode Island Interscholastic League was formed, and the puck had officially dropped on organized schoolboy hockey.

To grow up playing hockey in Quebec is to grow up dreaming of wearing Montreal Canadiens red, blue and white. Not surprisingly, Adelard dressed his teams in color schemes emulating those of the Habs. His successors—in particular, Larry Kish and Bill Belisle—would continue the tradition.

The rosters of those first Mount teams read like a lineup card from a Quebec junior hockey league: Charlebois, Bourgeois, Cournoyer, Boucher, Allard, Forget, Guaron, et al. The owners of such surnames played like semi-pro players from the environs of Quebec as well, and Adelard and Mount quickly became a power. Although Brother Adelard coached the Mounties in 1926, 1927, 1928 and 1940, he enjoyed prolific success after moving to the "front office" as director of hockey operations. Under Adelard's direction as team "general manager," MSC racked up ten state titles between 1933 and 1947, three New England titles (1934, 1935 and 1939) and three national titles (1935, 1939 and 1940). From 1932 through 1940, the Mount posted a record of 160–7–15. In retrospect, Brother Adelard could do nothing but win. The future "Father of Rhode Island Hockey" had the pedigree, the milieu, the players and, most important, the will to win.

Most Mount hockey alumni will tell you that over the ninety-year history of Mount Saint Charles hockey, few fans have rooted on the sticksters with more fervor than the Brothers of the Sacred Heart. This spirit of competition began, of course, with Brother Adelard, whose belief in loving thy neighbor rivaled his insistence on importing thy hockey neighbor from Quebec. With the help of his network of Canadian scouts, Adelard enticed/recruited some of the best Canadian hockey players to come to play at Mount, to earn a fine American education and to get a taste of the American (well, Anglo-Canadian) culture. Who'd notice that Mount was playing ringers? The imports looked like local kids, even talked like them—but when it came to playing, no one was in their league.

The success of the 1935 National Champion Mounties underscored the glaring disparity in talent between MSC and the competition. The squad opened the preseason with a 20–0 win over North High School, Worcester County champion. Other contenders fared no better. Mount beat its first six RIIL contenders by a combined 30–1 score and went on to record twelve shutouts that year. Only LaSalle played Mount competitively, losing just 2–0 late in the regular season and 4–0 in the championship game. The Mount polished off an easy New England title, thumping New Haven 8–1. They toppled Boston All-Stars 6–0 and New Rochelle (NY) 6–0 en route to their first national title. MSC finished the campaign 26–1, outscoring the opposition by an absurd 152–12 count. The starting lineup included three Canadian imports; in fact, of the sixteen players on the roster, ten were from Quebec. The legacy of the "Flying Frenchmen" was in the process of being written.

# The Birth and Evolution of Mount Saint Charles Hockey

As the decade came to a flying conclusion, hockey interest was at an all-time high. Crowds of over five thousand were commonplace at the Rhode Island Auditorium, the state's sole indoor hockey facility, as fanatics literally climbed the walls to see who could beat the Mighty Mounties. No one could touch MSC in 1939; the Mount went undefeated in league play and finished 23–1. Only a loss to the Boston College freshman team marred a perfect record. MSC outscored its opposition 108–22, and the all-state team sported all Mounties, a record that stands to this day. (The 1989 team, featuring the "Big Five," placed five players on the all-state team.) MSC topped the campaign with another New England and national title.

And so it went. Under Brother Adelard, MSC may have maintained its stranglehold on Rhode Island hockey indefinitely. But finally, those who skated against Adelard's clubs grew tired of losing. They sniffed for clues as to why MSC was dominant, and the clues led them to the fourth floor of the big, red-bricked building on Logee Street, which housed the school's boarders.

When officials at the Rhode Island Interscholastic League confirmed Mount's use of Canadian players, they passed a rule that required boarders to be residents of the school for one year before becoming eligible to play RIIL-sanctioned sports. Since most of Mount's Canadian players played only for one season, the ruling all but shut down Adelard's pipeline of übertalented Canadians.

Without his usual bounty of Canadian studs available to play for Mount, Adelard took matters into his own hands. He formed an independent team composed of Canadian players ineligible to play in the RIIL. He dubbed the club the "Flying Frenchmen" and cobbled a schedule against college teams and other amateur clubs. That season, the Frenchmen went 10–8–1, concluding their season with a loss to the Boston Junior Olympics in the New England Amateur Tournament.

Meanwhile, MSC was forced to regroup. With its core of Canadian players now skating with Brother Adelard's Flying Frenchmen prep team, MSC entered the 1940–41 season with just one returning player. The result: Mount finished the season 5–2–3 and just one point shy of a playoff spot.

MSC, however, was not through, even if it had been forced to rely on "local" talent. The Mount won state titles in 1942, 1945, 1946 and 1947. The 1947 team included a spark-plug forward named Normand "Bill" Belisle. Meanwhile, as the 1940s drew to a close, Mount hockey headed toward a lengthy dry spell. Burrillville High developed into a power, and LaSalle became another frequent title contender. Other programs such as Hope High and Cranston also produced solid programs as the RIIL expanded over the years. The Mount program needed a shot of Mount Pride to experience its hockey resurrection.

Part II

# THE RESURRECTION OF MOUNT PRIDE: THE LARRY KISH ERA

Chapter 3

# HOW THE FLYING FRENCHMEN BECAME THE FOUNDERING FRENCHMEN

By the end of the 1950s, a shift in power had occurred in Rhode Island hockey, and Mount no longer was the king of the ice rink. For instance, Hope High captured the 1959–60 state title by trumping Burrillville 4–1 and 2–1. However, the Broncos vindicated themselves by topping Hope 3–1 in the New England championships. Mount, meanwhile, finished the season with a 3–13–1 record, tallying only twenty goals in seventeen games.

Things continued to go downhill from there. In 1960–61, Mount entered the season with high hopes, but it finished the season 1–14–1, eighth in the nine-team league. That made their record over the last four seasons a dismal 10–51–5. Hope, meanwhile, captured its second straight title, with LaSalle winning the New England tourney.

The following year, Mike Lovett followed Don Girard as Mount head coach. Lovett was a former all-state Mount forward who brought to the program a system based on hard work and hard skating. His efforts paid dividends, as Mount registered its first winning season since 1955 (11–9) but finished in fifth place in the division. Meanwhile, Burrillville defeated LaSalle to win its eleventh state title in its twenty-one-year history.

Mount entered the 1962–63 season with experienced goaltending, high hopes and a new arena in the works. Despite the optimism, Mount finished the campaign on a five-game losing streak to post a 7–9 record. Burrillville remained hot, capturing both the state and New England titles. The 1963–64 season saw Mount skate in the newly dedicated Brother Adelard Arena, but despite the home-ice advantage, Mount missed the

Larry Tremblay was one of Mount's top players in the mid-1960s. He eventually became an assistant coach at MSC, but he's best known for commandeering the Moses Brown hockey program to state prominence. *Photo courtesy of Mount Saint Charles.*

playoffs and finished 8–12–1 overall. This time, Cranston East emerged as state champion.

The following year, Mount rebounded to make the playoffs, thanks to a 10–6–2 record that landed them in fourth place in the Metropolitan Conference. Their competition in the opening round was Suburban Conference champion Woonsocket High, in the inaugural matchup between the neighboring schools. Woonsocket proved to be the better team, sweeping aside MSC in two games of their best-of-three series to capture the "City Championship."

The Villa Novans then lost to Cranston East in three games; the Bolt that year was led by star forward Joe Cavanaugh, who won the scoring title with twenty-six goals and thirty-seven assists. Mount's top scorer, Bob Harnois, tallied ten goals and eight assists. Those comparatively modest stats underscore one of the problems Mount endured during the 1950s and '60s: weak offense. East, however, was upset by LaSalle, which had toppled Burrillville in the semifinals.

The 1965–66 season marked Lovett's last year at the Mount helm. Again, hopes were high as the Mounties returned an experienced club. The results

# The Resurrection of Mount Pride: The Larry Kish Era

weren't bad: 10–8–2 overall—fourth place in the Metropolitan Conference. In the playoffs, MSC blew past Warwick 10–0 and 7–0 to face Cranston East in the semifinals. East, which had already beaten Mount three times during the regular season, swept the Hilltoppers 4–1 and 9–0 before going on to win both state and New England championships. Once the Flying Frenchmen, Mount had become the Foundering Frenchmen.

## Chapter 4
# THE CREATION OF MOUNT PRIDE

The years of Mount's relative mediocrity would end quickly with the arrival of Larry Kish for the 1966–67 season. A former head coach at Cumberland High and star defenseman at Providence College, Kish in his six years as Mount head coach resurrected a once-proud program with a steady diet of skating seasoned with a dash of self-respect, Mount Pride and discipline. Kish's methods, in many ways, mirrored those of the oft-emulated Montreal Canadiens coaching staff.

"All that Mount Pride, Bill Belisle gets the credit," says Charlie Mandeville, a Mount captain on the 1967–68 state championship team and the author of *Mount Saint Charles Hockey: How It All Started*. "But it started when Larry Kish took over."

A native of Welland, Ontario, Kish, like Bill Belisle and Brother Adelard, drew up his hockey game plan from his own life and hockey experiences. His hockey career began in earnest when he left home at age fifteen to play for the Peterborough Petes, the major junior affiliate of the Montreal Canadiens. His first coach, working his first coaching assignment for the parent Habs, was Scotty Bowman, future Hall of Fame coach and winner of nine Stanley Cups, five with Montreal.

To be a Canadian teenager playing for the most respected hockey franchise in the world was enough to make any kid shake in his hockey boots. Kish was no different. Each of Bowman's practices was like Game 7 of the Stanley Cup finals in the third overtime of sudden death. With one bad pass or one missed check, Kish could have gotten the proverbial heave-ho. As a result, he stole a page out of the Habs' book on hockey propriety and became the perfect pupil.

"When I went away, I plagiarized the concepts of the Montreal Canadiens a lot," says Kish. "The little things—you always had to be dressed properly. If you left your jersey on the floor of the dressing room, they would cut you, send you packing. There was a fear there when you played. I was scared every day of the week that I wouldn't be able to stay there. I was the youngest guy on the team. I wanted to be a player so bad that I followed all the rules and regulations, whether it was shining your shoes or making your bed. They were pretty demanding in those days. The end result was that I carried that discipline with me my entire life."

By Kish's second season with the Petes, college scouts had begun to aggressively recruit the smooth-skating defenseman. Bowman, however, was not convinced that Kish had the size and strength to make it in the NHL. He offered advice that hardly sat well with the teenager.

"Scotty came to me and said, 'You're a little on the small side to play defense in pro hockey. If I were you, I'd be looking to get your college degree in your back pocket and take it where it goes from there.'"

Kish was crushed but heeded his coach's advice. With an eye toward a possible future in the American Hockey League, Kish enrolled at Providence College. Since the Canadiens' AHL farmhand, the Providence Reds, was a slap shot away, Kish figured he'd parlay his college career into a future with the Reds. Maybe one day he'd get a shot to skate with the big team at the professional cathedral of hockey, the Forum. At PC, Kish learned the value of humility, perseverance and pride. If the Montreal Canadiens effused hockey nobility, PC's hockey program was an infant struggling to stay on its own two feet. "I walked into Providence College, and when I got there, I said, 'Gee whiz, this is Mickey Mouse,'" says Kish.

At PC, Kish and his teammates struggled to get by on a pauper's hockey budget; they were saddled with used equipment and sometimes didn't even have tape for their hockey sticks. Sometimes they were short a few sticks. Practices were held at 6:00 a.m.—if the lights in the arena were working. Sometimes the players even practiced on a nearby pond. When the team needed supplies, Kish became team advocate, soliciting help from the neighboring Providence Reds or Springfield Indians of the American Hockey League. "I was blessed because I knew a number of players personally," says Kish. "[Future NHL defenseman] Barclay Plager played for the Springfield Indians, and I met him in Peterborough along with Jacques Caron, who was the goalie in Springfield. I would see these guys, and they would take care of me. If Eddie Shore was giving away anything at end of the night, I always had sticks around. [We] never had black tape or white tape; you just picked up whatever you could. Some kids from Rhode Island had a bit more, and their parents would bring things in and share them."

The Friars may have gone to battle dressed and equipped like paupers, but under the direction of legendary coach Tom Eccleston, Kish became one of the top rearguards ever to play for the program.

When Kish came to Mount, he vowed to do things a bit differently than at PC. Still, he found the Mount hockey program "wasn't in really good shape prior to us getting in there. We didn't allow too much grass to grow under our feet, and we got things going."

Fortunately, Kish had ample support from the academy, the booster club and future Smithfield coaching guru Reynolds Lillibridge. Kish's hockey itinerary included a schedule heavy on college freshmen teams that would challenge his players both physically and mentally. He felt he could use a "home" arena such as Brother Adelard Arena to attract top-flight players from within and beyond the Rhode Island borders. Most important, however, was Kish's emphasis on hockey basics. "The most important thing to me for kids that age was skating," Kish says. "You had to be able to skate. I put an awful lot of time into the skills and levels of skating. I always felt we skated better than most of the teams in those days. And where did that come from? It came from Montreal; when they were winning Stanley Cups, it was their speed—their ability to be half a step quicker."

Kish also recognized the correlation between success in the classroom and on the ice. To that end, he made study hall a mandatory component of his players' training.

"Larry Kish had high standards, including discipline," says John Harwood, who played three seasons under Kish. "He was an English teacher, and he didn't want dumb hockey players. Each day at 2:30 was study hall until 3:30, and then we were on the ice at 4:00. If you didn't show up at study hall, you didn't practice. No long hair. On the ice, he was a drill sergeant."

"Study hall…I just felt it gave the kids an incentive," explains Kish. "You had players, at least in the first stage of the program, like John Harwood, who had to work so hard academically but did really well in the classroom. Jimmy King was also a good student. When you had kids like that who were doing well academically, it really made the other kids do the same thing. They looked up to John, and they looked up to some of these other players. Not only were they good players, but they were also doing well academically. It rubbed off. The parents that put their faith and trust in MSC, including myself, they were counting on us to do a job, and I think that, for the most part, we did a pretty good job."

Kish also believed that players, like business executives, dressed for success. He made his players wear ties on game day and introduced windbreakers and duffel bags in the Mount colors. Even red-white-and-blue skates made an appearance. When a Kish-coached Mount team arrived at an arena for a game, it did so in style.

"People in the lobby stopped and looked at us the first time they saw blue blazers with 'Mounties' on it," recalls Mandeville. "His thing was that if people perceive you as good, people can be intimidated, and that gives you an advantage. If you do anything, do it with class."

Kish's first season at the helm began auspiciously, thanks to contributions from players who would lead MSC to its first state title a year later. The season opener versus LaSalle went to Mount when Charlie Mandeville's attempted pass from behind the Rams' net to teammate Bob Martin caromed off all-state goalie Tim Reagan and into the net. A 2–0 loss to Burrillville did not derail the Mounties, who followed up with a 5–0 defeat of defending state and New England champion Cranston East. It was the Bolt's first loss after twenty-three straight RIIL wins. Again, the trio of Bob Martin, Bill Cooper and Mandeville contributed key points to the win. A 2–1 win over traditional Maine power St. Dominic's followed. And so the Mounties were off and running in 1966–67. They finished in second place with a record of 10–6–3, including a win and tie against East. MSC, however, could not buck back the Broncos that year; Burrillville took the regular-season series two games to one. Then, in the semifinals of the playoffs, fifth-seed Burrillville beat second-seed Mount 3–2. Cranston East went on to top LaSalle in the finals.

Compared to recent years, Mount's 10–6–3 record in 1966–67 was a huge step forward, especially up front. Unable to amass much offense in the last few seasons, MSC ended the season outscoring the opposition 87–31. Mandeville led the offense with nineteen goals and eleven assists. Unfortunately for Mount, eight seniors graduated from the 1966–67 club. Surely the loss of so many skilled players was a portent to a rebuilding 1967–68 season, the press and locals muttered. What few knew, however, was that an exceptional group of underclassmen waited in the wings.

Like Brother Adelard, Kish had no qualms about recruiting players, some from beyond the Rhode Island border. One of the first players he enticed to Mount was a future lawyer and Rhode Island Speaker of the House. John Harwood was a lanky, ginger-haired rink rat from Pawtucket who'd grown up a stone's throw from the locker rooms at the Rhode Island Auditorium.

When he wasn't depositing goals for his youth teams, Harwood swooned over the ambience of the hockey palace—the chicken wire above the dasher boards, the pall of smoke that hung over the ice and the more than seven thousand fans packing the old building to the rafters. Harwood had also seen Larry Kish play hockey. "I was twelve years old, and I watched him play at PC. He was one of the greatest defensemen I ever saw," recalls Harwood.

At age twelve, however, Harwood entertained no dreams of playing for the Mount franchise or for Kish—that is, until Kish met with Harwood and his parents and convinced them that the Mount "would suit John just fine." In landing the gifted forward, Kish promised the Harwood family he would transport their son to and from school. So, each day for four years, Kish made the circuitous trip from his home in Providence to the Harwoods' home in Pawtucket and then on to Woonsocket. The trek symbolized the lengths to which Kish would travel to support his team and players.

"Harwood was the first shining star—a great athlete," says Kish. "He wasn't the world's greatest skater. He had to work hard to get where he was on the ice. He was probably the most intelligent person with the puck, and he knew how to make plays. He was a playmaker and had a great intestinal fortitude, and that's what made John what he is today. John was like a brother and son to me. I picked him up every day of the week for four years, and that was a promise I made to the family. That's how we did things at the Mount in those days."

The Mount faithful quickly became acquainted with Harwood and reacquainted with seasoned veterans such as Charlie Mandeville and Bob Martin. Mount quickly recorded nine wins and jumped into first place four points ahead of Burrillville, next up on the schedule. For two periods, Burrillville and Mount looked like two prizefighters tied up against the ropes and unable to land a clear punch. The Broncos' speed and tight checking limited Mount to just a few shots on goal through two periods. In the third stanza, however, Mandeville rescued his club by beating BHS goalie Guy Morse (five saves) at 3:49. Joe Butera added a goal two minutes later, and MSC rode the solid goaltending of Kevin Littlefield (twelve saves) to its tenth straight win.

By now, the Mount Saint Charles hockey program and its players had returned to their vaunted throne not only atop Logee Street but also at the apex of the town and its culture. Players such as Martin and Harwood and Littlefield had once again donned their superman robes to fly above the city. The townspeople, who hungered for a championship, were happy to canonize them.

# The Resurrection of Mount Pride: The Larry Kish Era

"We would go to Beaupre's Pharmacy," recalls Mandeville, now in his early sixties. "They would come up and say, 'You're Charlie Mandeville; I saw you play hockey.' Everywhere you went, people would know who you were. [We were] a bunch of kids playing the game of hockey, giving something special to the town."

Despite the air of confidence and excitement that held the city in an icy embrace, Mount still had to complete its season. Cranston East skated into Adelard Arena primed to avenge its early-season loss to the Mounties. They didn't disappoint the Cranston faithful, toppling MSC 3–2 before a raucous crowd of 1,500. Once again, Mandeville and Harwood led the Mounties on the scoring sheet. Despite the loss, Mount remained in first place, two points ahead of The Bolt. MSC regained its equilibrium, briefly, to beat Woonsocket, 4–0, and Burrillville, 4–1. The trio of Bob Martin, Mandeville and Harwood led the Mounties in the big win over the Broncos. LaSalle handed Mount its second loss of the season, 4–0, but again MSC rebounded to beat Pilgrim and North Providence. On the docket next was Cranston East and a battle for the Met A Championship at the Rhode Island Auditorium.

For a while, East looked as if it had perfected the formula to beat MSC. Goals by Otto Tingley, Harvey Bennett and Ray Tiernan gave Cranston a 3–1 lead. However, Mount rallied to tie the game on goals by Harwood and Martin. The two teams, so close in talent and in the standings all year, took their battle to overtime. This game came down to special teams. With his club on the power play, Mandeville slammed home the rebound of Martin's shot to provide MSC with a 4–3 win and its first Metropolitan title since 1945. The win also earned the Mounties an automatic bye into the state finals.

After slipping past Cranston East in the quarterfinals and Burrillville in the semis, LaSalle prepared to face off against Mount in what would become a historic championship series. Game 1 went to the Mounties, 2–1, in double overtime when Bob Cooper took Harwood's pass and drilled a slapper past LaSalle goalie Tim Reagan.

There are moments when the Mount sweater and its aura can magically transform a vulnerable flesh-and-blood teenager into a superhero. Such was the case for Charlie Mandeville. As his team readied itself before the start of Game 2, Mandeville was "scared shitless." But then he donned the hallowed Mount uniform, laced his skates and grabbed his gloves and stick, and he and his teammates took the ice at the Aud to a thunderous rendition of "When the Saints Go Marching In" from the Mount Pep Band. There were over six thousand fans hanging from the ceiling and practically the chicken wire that ran atop and along the boards. Suddenly, Mandeville was Superman—with Mount Pride swelling in his chest and his teammates equally sky high.

Mount looked as if it would quickly and easily put the Rams away in Game 2. Mandeville scored just fifteen seconds into the contest. After the Rams tied the contest, Mount's Don Mountford and Harwood gave the Hilltoppers a 3–1 lead. With MSC skating well and goalie Kevin Littlefield at the top of his game, Mount appeared headed to victory. The Rams, however, had Reagan, the state's best goalie, and in the third period rallied to knot the game at three. Harwood, however, scored what Mount fans thought would be the game-winning goal with fifty-five seconds left in regulation. In keeping with the ebb and flow of the game and series, LaSalle's Paul Driscoll tied the game at four with just seconds remaining in overtime. The teams battled through two scoreless overtimes before officials stopped the game. In a harbinger of the epic 1988 Mount-Hendricken "five-game" best-of-three championship series, Game 2 of the 1968 Mount-LaSalle series was officially declared a non-game, to be replayed two nights later.

With nearly six thousand fans packing every inch of the Auditorium, LaSalle prevailed over Mount, 5–3, to officially win Game 2 and knot the series at one game apiece. Harwood had a pair of goals and Mandeville one, but behind Reagan's stonewall goaltending, LaSalle raced to victory by breaking open a 2–2 game in the second period.

By the time the two teams took the ice for the deciding game of the series, they had already played thirteen periods of hockey, including four extra periods, in a span of six days. Mount, however, needed no extra time to close the book on the 1967–68 championship. Harwood, Leo Bush and Al Lavallee gave MSC a three-goal lead that LaSalle could not overcome. A late third-period goal spoiled Littlefield's shutout bid, but MSC emerged with a 3–1 win and its first state championship in twenty-one seasons. Harwood was named tournament MVP and his teammate Pat Lovett the Most Valuable Defenseman. LaSalle's Reagan earned Best Goalie honors.

After a two-decade title drought, Mount's 1967–68 championship was a victory not just for the school but also for the city, its people and its culture. Although MSC would lose to Berlin High of New Hampshire in the first round of the New England Championships, Mount Pride had been reestablished under Kish.

"Culturally, '68 was a shock," says Harwood. "It was a rebirth of pride instilled in the old-timers [those who had followed the program for years]. We were the George Washington of the program of the modern-day era." The *Woonsocket Call* newspaper celebrated Mount's title by posting in the windows of its building copies of the articles that recounted the title-clinching game. Kish recalls:

> *It was a rallying point for sure in Woonsocket. Woonsocket was a mill town, a place where people worked hard for what they had. It wasn't a very affluent area. Woonsocket had a strong French Canadian base, and when you coached players like I did in the pros who were of French descent, more than any other nationality that played the game, it was their strong family values and their loyalty. It's very evident; all you have to do is look at the Montreal Canadiens to see how big hockey is to the French population in the province of Quebec. It's astounding how deeply rooted it is. To me, that was the start of the rebirth of schoolboy hockey in terms of putting people in the seats. We were not well liked; the Cranston Easts and LaSalles were not too pleased with us. We were like the kid who came down from the woods in Woonsocket, and they were saying, "Where did these guys come from?" For us, it was an opportunity to build a little bit of community pride. We became a real cornerstone of pride in Woonsocket, for sure.*

The 1968 season provided a few intriguing footnotes. For starters, Mandeville and Harwood were named to the all-state first team, along with LaSalle's Reagan, Ashley Atherton of Cranston East and Joe Mousseau and Walt Sitko of Burrillville. Harwood led the Mounties in scoring with twenty-two goals and twenty-five assists, while Mandeville posted twenty-two goals and seventeen assists and Martin eleven goals and ten assists. The team outscored its opposition 105–45 and concluded the campaign 22–4–2 overall. Harwood's 47 points placed him second in the league in scoring behind Joe Mousseau—maybe. More than forty-five years later, Harwood, Mandeville and even Kish contested the final scoring statistics. Mandeville recalls:

> *In 1968, John Harwood's sophomore year, Harwood was playing against [Burrillville coach] Babe Mousseau's son for the scoring title. The next day, Larry Kish looks at the box score, and there's Joe Mousseau, Babe's son, assisted on the second goal. Kish remembers that Joe wasn't on the ice! The* Providence Journal *hired high school kids to call in game scores. Babe's daughters were covering games at Levy (Rink), and they would put their brother's name on there [the score sheet]—pad it. At the end of the year, he beats John Harwood for the scoring title and makes all-state. Larry Kish finds out and calls the* Providence Journal. *Larry didn't have real*

*proof. Next year, the* Providence Journal *was scrutinizing everything, and Joe Mousseau wasn't even in the scoring race.*

Today, Harwood waxes coy about the scoring "scandal." "I knew who won it," he says. "I found out what happened."

For the next two seasons, there was no doubt who won the state scoring title: John Harwood. With Harwood and other talented underclassmen beginning to fill its stable, the Mount machine was just beginning to roll.

Despite the graduation of top players such as Bob Martin, Charlie Mandeville and Joe Butera, Mount returned a bounty of talent for the 1968–69 campaign. Harwood, now a junior, led the offense, with Pat Lovett back at defense and Kevin Littlefield back to man the pipes. New players were expected to play key roles, and the hockey mavens, unlike the previous year, expected the Mounties to make a run for the state title.

MSC did not disappoint—for a while, at least.

A high-powered offense led The Mount to four straight wins to open the season. Perennial power Cranston East followed, led by stars Harvey Bennett and Otto Tingley. This time, the Bolt triumphed 1–0 and lifted Cranston East into a first-place tie with the Mounties. MSC followed the defeat by beating Maine powers Waterville High School and St. Dominic's in a holiday tournament. Then the Hilltoppers toppled previously undefeated LaSalle 5–3. Easy victories over non-contenders helped boost Mount's record to 10–1. The Mounties' winning skein ended with a 2–1 loss to LaSalle; still, with big wins over Burrillville and Cranston East, Mount went on to win the Metropolitan Division regular-season title. The title earned them an automatic berth in the state finals—eventually. With both the quarterfinals and semifinals series best-of-three games, Mount was forced to sit and watch.

Whether the long layoff affected Mount's performance is a matter of conjecture. Either way, Cranston East, which had topped Burrillville and LaSalle to reach the finals, had its way with the Mounties. The Bolt blew the Mount away with three first-period goals en route to a stunning 5–1 victory. Game 2 ended in a 3–3 double-overtime tie, forcing the teams back to the ice at the Rhode Island Auditorium to face off one more time in Game 2. Again, East left no doubt. Otto Tingley's goal fifty-one seconds into the opening period sent the Bolt on their way to a 3–0 win, the state title and, later, the New England Championship.

After finishing the 1968–69 season on a disappointing note, Mount entered the 1969–70 season with the potential to dominate the competition. Harwood was back for his senior season, along with Lovett, Cooper, goalie

# The Resurrection of Mount Pride: The Larry Kish Era

Dick Imondi and a strong supporting cast that included future Boston Bruin Tom Songin. Add to the mix speedy forward Jimmy King, who had transferred to Mount from Vermont Academy midway through the previous season, and Mount had the ingredients for one of the most powerful offenses in its history.

Mount sprang into first place by topping Burrillville twice and defending state champ Cranston East. LaSalle was no match, losing to MSC 5–0. Through its first ten games, MSC was undefeated, and Harwood, King and Cooper were wreaking havoc in opposing teams' defensive zones. The Mount juggernaut pounded its competition and improved to 19–0, looking unbeatable and unstoppable. But MSC came down to earth, briefly, with 4–3 losses to Warwick and Cranston East. No problem. The Mounties' 19–2 record earned them the regular-season Metropolitan title—and in impressive form. Harwood officially won his second straight scoring title with twenty-two goals and thirty-eight assists. Cooper, King and Lovett all recorded at least thirty-point seasons. Six other players tallied at least 10 points apiece. Harwood and Cooper were named to the first-team all-state team. Gary Schofield and King earned second-team honors, and Dave Charron placed on the Honorable Mention team.

The championship best-of-three series pitted defending champion Cranston East against Mount. In Game 1, MSC rode goals from Cooper (two), Lovett, Paul Fredette and Harwood into a 5–1 lead after two periods. The Bolt refused to succumb without a fight. Goals from Jackie Lester, Len Alsfeld and Bill Bennett drew East to within one goal, at 5–4. But Cranston could not beat Imondi (eight saves) with the game-tying goal, as MSC prevailed behind a forty-six-shot attack.

In Game 2, Cooper led the Mounties with a hat trick while King and Dick Goryl potted single goals as Mount rode a forty-four-shot assault to win 5–1 and record its second state title under Larry Kish. MSC went on to beat Waterville High (Maine) 5–2 to win the New England Championship as well. Harwood was the star, with three goals in the title contest.

It had been a magical season…but it soon became an unforgettable nightmare.

At the conclusion of the 1967–68 season, the Principals Committee on Athletics approved a rule that forced athletes to disclose receipt of financial aid. Due to an administrative oversight, MSC had failed to inform the Interscholastic League that during the 1968–69 season, one of its players had received $250 in aid. The league acted upon that information in 1970, stripping the 1969–70 team of its regular-season and state championship titles. It also placed the Mount program on probation for the 1970–71 season and barred the Mounties from participating in postseason play that year. The league did allow MSC to retain its New England title, however.

The Mount Saint Charles community was stunned. In his book *Mount Saint Charles Academy: How It All Started*, author and former Mountie Charlie Mandeville questioned the veracity of the Principal's Committee: "The real reason was that the Rhode Island Coaches Association (spearheaded by Burrillville coach Babe Mousseau) threatened to form their own league if the Principals Committee did not stop the alleged recruiting of players by Mount Saint Charles."

The stringent penalties enforced by the league may have cost MSC a state title, but this did not dissuade other talented players from enrolling at Mount. "The next thing we know, we started to develop a reputation, and we started to get players to come from Massachusetts and all over the place that became a part of the program," says Kish. "I think the results speak for themselves; we had great results, and we weren't very well liked. There were issues within the state where [others had said] we weren't doing things the right way and 'we ought to penalize these guys because they've gotten too good.' It was kind of interesting, to say the least."

Another of Kish's coveted trophies was a kid who would for years be a fixture at Mount. Tony Ciresi, a resident of Cranston, was a freshman goalie playing for prep school power Deerfield Academy in Deerfield, Massachusetts, when he experienced a Mount hockey epiphany during the 1967–68 Mount-LaSalle finals. "In ninth grade, I was at the Auditorium watching Mount and LaSalle," Ciresi remembers. "Tim Reagan [was] the best goalie ever. LaSalle was favored until John Harwood lit it up for two games, double overtime. That's when it started—Mount Pride."

Meanwhile, Kish liked what he saw in the tall, cool, immensely talented netminder, and he aggressively courted Ciresi. Ciresi transferred to Mount for his junior season, at which point he joined another talented goalie, sophomore Kevin McCabe. For two seasons, the pair composed arguably the best goaltending tandem ever to play at Mount. They backboned the Mounties during the 1970–71 campaign, in which Mount posted an 18–3 record and captured the Metropolitan regular-season title. With Mount ineligible for postseason play, Burrillville, which had beaten MSC three times during the regular season, beat LaSalle to win its thirteenth state title in the history of the program.

In the fall of 1971, the Rhode Island Principals Committee on Athletics lifted the Mount hockey suspension; Mount was back in business, and its players, especially Ciresi, were bent on dethroning archrival Burrillville. The

# The Resurrection of Mount Pride: The Larry Kish Era

Mounties began the 1971–72 campaign with an easy win over Woonsocket. But when they faced off against powerful East Providence with future NHL coach Ron Wilson, along with Brad Wilson and Tom Army, the Mounties emerged with a hard-fought 4–4 tie. Two easy wins followed, and then MSC lined up against the Broncos. Burrillville made it four straight (including three straight wins over MSC in 1971) by toppling the Mounties 4–3 at Levy Arena. MSC rebounded with wins over Woonsocket, Pilgrim and talented LaSalle and headed into the LaSalle Christmas tournament at Thayer Arena on the upswing. MSC's first opponent: Burrillville.

By this point, the Broncos coaches and players had perfected a system to stifle the Mount's powerful offense. Burrillville also had the firepower to match MSC line for line. Burrillville put together another A-plus performance in thumping Mount 5–1 in the opener of the tourney. Still, just a few weeks and numerous wins later, MSC was in first place by one point over EP and two over both LaSalle and Burrillville.

A 3–3 tie with LaSalle sent Mount on a six-game winning streak with Burrillville riding into town. This time, MSC pulled in the reins and stopped the Broncos 3–0, with Ciresi earning the shutout with eighteen saves. Mount ended the regular season with a 5–1 win over LaSalle and a 4–3 loss to Burrillville. Still, MSC captured the Metropolitan regular-season title and therefore earned a bye into the finals of the championship series. With playoff series wins over East Providence and Cranston East, Burrillville earned the right to play Mount for the state title.

After beating MSC in five of their previous six meetings, Burrillville entered the finals favored slightly. However, Game 1 of the best-of-three series went to Mount, 2–1, thanks in large part to Ciresi's acrobatics and twenty-three saves. Andy Cote and Joe Rego paced the offense with a goal apiece. Game 2 was played before a sellout crowd of 5,525 at the Rhode Island Auditorium. Unlike the opener, Game 2 was an offensive slugfest. Future Boston Bruin forward Tom Songin scored twice in the second period, and the Mounties fought off a pair of Broncos rallies en route to a 6–4 win and their twelfth state title.

That's where the season should have ended if you were a Mount fan and player, especially goalie Tony Ciresi. After battling all season and throughout the finals, Mount and Burrillville days later met in the New England Championships. This time, Burrillville rallied to beat MSC 3–1 before falling in the finals to Waterville High of Maine. The defeat was Mount's sixth in nine contests against the Broncos. Despite winning the state championship and being named a second-team all-state all-

Tony Ciresi was tending goal for a Massachusetts prep school when Larry Kish recruited him to MSC. Here, the Mount goalie follows action during the 1972 state finals against Burrillville High School. *Photo courtesy of Tony Ciresi.*

star, the loss to Burrillville in the NE championships still bothers Ciresi. "Burrillville was clearly our biggest rival when I was there," says Ciresi "My senior year, we beat them for the state championship, but they beat us in Lewiston, Maine, to knock us out of the New England Championship. That was my most bitter high school memory."

# THE RESURRECTION OF MOUNT PRIDE: THE LARRY KISH ERA

It was one of the few negative memories from his hockey career. After graduating from Mount, Ciresi attended the University of Pennsylvania. Years later, he served as head coach of North Smithfield High and Woonsocket High. Most folks remember Ciresi as a Mount assistant coach from 1980 to 1990.

"Playing at Mount Saint Charles was the best time of my life," says Ciresi, today a teacher and goalie coach for the Brown University men's hockey team. "We were the big fish in a little pond; there were packed houses, and

Mount goalie Tony Ciresi sweeps aside the puck during Mount's 2–1 Game 1 victory over Burrillville High in the 1972 finals. *Photo courtesy of Tony Ciresi.*

we won championships. My senior year we played a fifty-six-game season that included college freshmen teams. Coaching was very enjoyable. I have ten championship jackets. The highlight was working with these kids; I worked with some who are still friends now."

# The Resurrection of Mount Pride: The Larry Kish Era

Meanwhile, Mount's loss to Burrillville in the New England Championship marked not only the end of Ciresi's career but also the end of Kish's coaching reign at MSC. Even before he accepted the coaching job at Mount, Kish's long-term goal was to be an athletic director at a major college program. With the intention to leave the academy after his sixth season, Kish pursued the highly coveted AD job at Boston College. "I had made up my mind that I had done everything I could at MSC and it was time to do something else," Kish says. "Was I cocky? I felt I was going to be the first person in the history of Boston College to be a Canadian and coach at that program. They picked Len Ceglarski, and I didn't get the job. But I had made up my mind I wasn't going back to MSC, and I ended up going to the Eastern League, and that was it."

The following year, Kish stood behind the bench of the Eastern Hockey League's Rhode Island Eagles. The team and league offered a small step up the coaching ladder for Kish. Even though the Eagles played their home games at Brother Adelard Arena, a hub for hockey, neither the town nor the state paid much attention to the team. Mount was the king of the ice rink.

Nonetheless, Kish parlayed the experience with the Eagles into a solid professional hockey coaching career, working in the Hartford Whalers and Edmonton Oilers systems.

Despite Kish's departure, the future of the Mount program appeared bright, thanks to a developing youth program, the Rhode Island Kings. Not only did Kish believe in recruiting top talent, but he was also sold on building a superior farm system that would continue to pipeline future Mounties for years to come. The Kings youth teams combined the vision of Kish with the superior coaching of another hockey maven, Bill Belisle. Kish recalls:

> *We got together, and we decided we were going to start our own Rhode Island youth program, the Rhode Island Kings* [the forerunner to the Woonsocket North Stars]. *And that program was really the program that fed the high school long-term. Not all the kids played in that program, but we became very, very good, and Billy did a great job with some of the other coaches we had. We had insulated that whole program with that youth hockey deal. He used to be able to bring really good players into the program and develop them into really good high school players but also really good collegiate players and pretty darn good pros.*
>
> *When I was coaching at the Mount, the players will tell you that we spent so much time skating, and Billy Belisle carried it on. He agreed with me when we were running those little youth league programs that speed kills, and it does—there's no substitute. I think we made them better players…we made them better skaters. We start slowly, but when we got to Christmas, we were just a better team because of our speed.*

Chapter 5

# SKATING THROUGH RUSSIA TO GET TO WOONSOCKET

The 1972–73 season introduced a new head coach, former North Smithfield coach Bernie Tobin, and a new assistant coach, Bill Belisle. The new coaching tandem entered the campaign with numerous holes in their roster, thanks to the graduation of Ciresi, Kilduff and Songin, among others. McCabe was back to man the pipes. By most standards, Mount's 17–6–2 record that year was solid. But by Mount standards, finishing third in the Met Division and then falling to Cranston West in the second round of the playoffs was a far cry from the '71–'72 state title. Furthermore, Burrillville, Mount's chief foe for the previous decade, went on to win its fourteenth state title and fourth New England championship.

While many of Kish's clubs featured players recruited from the Boston area, many of the players who composed Mount's 1973–74 squad hailed from Woonsocket and had risen through the town's excellent youth system. Among the cast were John Belisle, son of assistant Bill Belisle, and Don Choquette, future head coach at Cumberland High School. Led by the Woonsocket kids, Mount finished third in the Met A division in the regular season (17–6) but lost to eventual New England champ Burrillville in the quarterfinals. Burrillville may have won the NE's, but Cranston West captured the state title, topping BHS in a sweep.

In two years, Tobin had led the Mount to thirty-four wins and a pair of third-place finishes. Solid results, certainly, but not up to Kish's previous standards.

"Mr. Tobin was a great man and smart person in his own right, but he had a different style," says former Mountie John Belisle. "He…was an aggressive, tough coach in that he liked to hit on every play. He was not that strategic in terms of style of play or designing plays. The team did get disorganized, for lack of better word, and wasn't attracting the talent it used to, and we started to lose dominance quickly and head down to the bottom of the league. Mr. Tobin was a good man…but I think he wasn't in the right element there in terms of high school. I think if he coached older kids that were more knowledgeable and had more skills…he kind of let us do our own thing to a certain extent."

Exit Bernie Tobin; enter Steve Shea.

If Brother Adelard is considered the "Father of Rhode Island Hockey," it wouldn't be a stretch to call Stephen Shea the "biological father" of Mount girls hockey. Shea's daughters—Courtney (2009) and twins Caitlin and Allison (2012) played hockey for MSC for nearly half of the program's twelve-year history. All were captains of their teams, top point producers and leaders from early on in their careers. Shea, assistant coach for three seasons under Amy McGuire, led the Mount girls to the 2011–12 state title. He retired from coaching after the 2012 season but has been an English teacher at the academy since 1974. Shea's son Brendan, a speedy forward, captained the Mount boys' hockey team in 2006 and was named to the all-state team. Those who have followed the Mount boys program since the Kish era, however, recall a different chapter in Steve Shea's coaching career—one that may go down as one of the most innovative and unique in the history of the Mount hockey program.

Chapter one of Shea's hockey biography begins in September 1972, when Shea was an undergraduate student and talented hockey player at Brown University. With the United States and the Soviet Union frozen in the summit of their political Cold War, hockey fanatics such as Shea eagerly awaited the world's first international battle between the NHL's elite players and the amateur greats from the Soviet Union: The Summit Series, Team Canada versus the Soviet Union. It was a battle not just between teams but between nations and ideologies: the Free World versus Communism; "Us" versus "Them."

Team Canada entered the series a heavy favorite, at least according to the myriad hockey mavens in North America. After all, the NHL was the world's elite league, and Team Canada boasted name brands such as Phil Esposito, Frank Mahovlich, Stan Mikita and Jean Ratelle. Head coach Harry Sinden tabbed Tony Esposito and Ken Dryden, future hall of famers, to guard the pipes. Then there was the least heralded line, consisting of Bobby Clarke, Paul Henderson and Ron Ellis, a *troika* that, ultimately, figured heavily in the series.

# The Resurrection of Mount Pride: The Larry Kish Era

The Soviets, meanwhile, were a curiosity to most Western fans and media gurus. Soviet players passed the puck ad nauseam and with military precision; instead of relying on slap shots from the point, which Canadian rearguards were accustomed to blocking, Soviet defensemen calmly held the puck and awaited a clear shot on goal or dished off to another player. Their defensemen jumped into the play, and their forwards crisscrossed in the neutral zone. Soviet hockey was, in a nutshell, dizzying in contrast to the linear NHL paradigm. Perhaps least appreciated by Team Canada's players and coaches was the individual talent boasted by the Soviet team. Goalie Vladislav Tretiak would, within the next few years, be recognized as one of the best goalies in the world; the feisty Boris Mickhailov was an offensive force; and Valery Kharlamov was to Soviet hockey what Wayne Gretzky would become to the NHL.

The Soviets needed little time to open the eyes of their Canadian counterparts. Game 1, played in Canada, went to the Soviet Union, 7–3, with Kharlamov potting two goals. Team Canada rallied to win Game 2, 4–1, but after forging a 4–4 tie, the Soviets won the fourth and final game played in Canada, 5–3. Throughout much of the fourth game, played in Vancouver, frustrated Team Canada fans serenaded the equally aggravated Canadian players with rousing choruses of boos. Minutes after the final horn, a sweaty and exasperated Phil Esposito responded by questioning the loyalty of the fans with a historic two-minute-and-thirty-second television interview conducted at center ice.

The Soviets had out-skated, outmuscled and out-performed the pros from North America. Moreover, the Soviets' style had gotten into the collective psyche of Team Canada. While Team Canada favored a dump-and-chase, heavy-hitting game, the Soviets shied away from the physical component. Instead, they used their sticks to jab, spear, derail and thwart Team Canada—often with a stick in the ribs, behind the knee or on the ankle.

Esposito, Clarke and Henderson were vocal in their disdain for the Soviets and the use of their sticks a la swords. The Soviets, meanwhile, decried the Canadians' physical play, especially from Bruins forward Wayne Cashman. Cashman had made his presence known in Game 2; in Game 3, he received a pair of slashing calls plus a ten-minute misconduct. With the war of emotions at a fever pitch, the Soviet Union captured Game 5, rallying from a 3–0 deficit to win 5–4 despite a heroic effort from Henderson. Henderson played much of the game with a concussion after sprawling heavily into the boards. But despite having his bell rung, Henderson tallied twice and added an assist.

Entering Game 6, Team Canada found itself forced to win the final three games in order to clinch the series. By this point, Sinden realized that the team's NHL-oriented dump-and-chase offensive system would not work against the Soviets. Esposito and his teammates also recognized that in order to beat the Russians, they would have to stop reacting to the Soviets' incessant stick work. They'd also have to lasso Kharlamov, whose brilliant skating and stickhandling was tattering Team Canada's defense. Sinden took the lead by switching to a puck-control offense that paid dividends. The Canadians took Game 6, 3–2. Unfortunately, this historic contest will be remembered for the shockingly poor officiating and the slash heard around the world. The two West German referees assessed thirty-one minutes in penalties to Team Canada versus just four for the Russians. The potpourri of whistles included a slashing minor and ten-minute major on Clarke, a major for high-sticking to Esposito and coincidental bench penalty. Officials also blew calls, such as the violent elbow Peter Mahovlich connected with Kharlamov's chin.

The incident that punctuated the ill will between both teams and nations occurred in the second period when Clarke broke Kharlamov's ankle with a vicious slash. Clarke's vicious two-hander, ordered by Team Canada assistant coach John Ferguson, sidelined arguably the best player in the game for most of the remainder of the series. With an ailing Kharlamov sidelined for Game 7, the Canadians, finally playing like an NHL all-star unit and showing championship form, topped the Soviets 4–3. Henderson again scored the game-winning goal. The penultimate game, however, featured a pair of controversial incidents. The first came late in the first period when Esposito was whistled for crosschecking Boris Mikhailov. At this point in the series, Esposito had had his fill with Mikhailov and, according to Espo, the Russian's stick work. From the penalty box, Esposito panned the ice, spotted Mikhailov and ran his finger across his throat, waved his fists and pointed at the Russian as if to say, "Let's battle."

Mikhailov did battle, but with Gary Bergman. Late in the third period, the pair mixed it up along the sideboards. With the brawnier Bergman enjoying the advantage, Mikhailov responded by using his skate as a weapon, bloodying Bergman's ankle with a pair of violent kicks. Bergman ended the fracas by slamming the Russian's head into the "chicken wire" that ran atop the boards at the Luzhniki Ice Palace.

Notwithstanding the on-ice fisticuffs, for Paul Henderson, the Summit Series proved to be the summit of his career. After scoring the game-winning goals in the previous two games, Henderson scored with thirty-four seconds left in Game 8 to give Team Canada a 6–5 victory and the Summit Series championship.

## The Resurrection of Mount Pride: The Larry Kish Era

While Henderson and his teammates celebrated the historic win, Steve Shea pondered the Summit Series from a different perspective. He eschewed the violence and the overtly physical play of Team Canada. Meanwhile, Shea marveled at the innovative style employed by the Soviets—images of the prolific passing, precision skating and superior stamina weaved their way into Shea's hockey fiber. "The Summit Series...the violence, Esposito and Clarke and wanting to kill the Russians...because of that, I became so anti–North American style hockey. I feel vindicated all these years later," says Shea.

Two years later, Shea left his teacher's position at Brewster Academy in New Hampshire to take over the Mount hockey program. He came to Woonsocket knowing little about MSC but a great deal about Russian hockey. "I had been at Adelard once when I was playing with Brown," Shea recalls. "They had a game scheduled against Dartmouth, whose rink had a smaller ice surface. To prepare for the game, the coach took them to practice at Mount. I couldn't wait to get out of there—what a dump!"

Ironically, Shea not only accepted the Mount gig, but he also grabbed the head coaching job of the Brown University women's hockey team. By Thanksgiving of 1974, Shea was pulling double duty between the two coaching jobs. Nonetheless, he entered the 1974–75 season thrilled to introduce the Russian style of hockey, which he hoped would help to right a Mount ship that lacked leadership and discipline and was listing badly. "I knew up front that it was a rough program and that they wanted me to clean up the language and misuse of substances," recalls Shea. "Keeping players involved...I couldn't afford to lose any kids/players. It was an in-between stage at Mount, and we were trying to build up the program."

Having grown up playing roller hockey on the streets of New York City, the innovative Shea had little trouble engaging the interest of his young protégés. He created drills designed to improve player coordination, one of which had him throwing tennis balls around the ice and another going one-on-six against his players.

"They could never catch me," chuckles Shea.

Or catch up with his system. Bill Belisle, Shea's assistant, whose coaching system is based on basics such as head-manning the puck, skating hard, back-checking, staying in lanes and so forth, was befuddled by the weaving Russian style. Early in their coaching relationship, Belisle discussed with Shea his reservation for working in a non-linear system.

"Steve, you don't need me as an assistant coach because I don't know anything about your Russian style," Belisle told Shea.

"Well, Coach, put it on paper," said Shea, nonchalantly. He then produced five pages of notes and diagrams that showed players crisscrossing each other and weaving up and down the ice. Belisle scanned the plays as if they were in a foreign language.

"Oh, shit—I can't understand that,'" Belisle told Shea, with a good-natured chuckle. "What the hell do you mean? Cross over here, swings back, the defenseman cuts behind on the other defenseman. Who's coming back? Steve, I read your illustrations, your notes; if you want to put up with me you can, but I really can't help you."

Shea, however, had complete confidence in Belisle.

"Oh, Coach, you'll understand it," he replied.

Belisle shrugged and simply said, "Okay." Like his players, Belisle did his utmost to work within Shea's vision and system. Yet neither the assistant coach nor the Mount players had the time or the wherewithal to successfully implement the Russian style in just one season.

John Guevremont, a defenseman on the 1975 and 1976 teams and now Shea's brother-in-law, recalls the buzz attendant to playing the Shea style:

> *Mr. Shea was way ahead of the curve. It was like, "Wow, this style is even better than the NHL style." It didn't seem all that crazy to us...rather than staying in your lane, the forwards did a lot of crisscrossing. I remember as a defenseman I kind of liked the idea: the puck dropped into the zone, and the two defensemen would drop back into the corners, and you would give it back and forth until you found someone. I just thought it was very well thought out. I think it was a great plan; I just don't think any of us were skillful enough to do it well. I have never had very good peripheral vision when it comes to sports, so I would look up and see everybody crisscrossing, and by the time I would start to pass it, he would be done crisscrossing. I just wasn't very good at it.*

"I loved Mr. Shea. When I was a junior, he was young, energetic and had wonderful ideas," says John Belisle, who played for Tobin, Shea and his father, Bill. "In terms of what he wanted do, in terms of Russian style, playing on off-wing, we had all sorts of crazy drills like the Russians did. We did all these things to improve coordination. Looking back, it was too much to expect from high school kids. He was a kind and caring coach, but I think he asked too much of high school kids because we hadn't even learned the fundamentals yet."

The 1974–75 season, the fiftieth anniversary of Mount hockey, began with a stunning 5–3 loss to Woonsocket in an Injury Fund game. It marked

# The Resurrection of Mount Pride: The Larry Kish Era

the Villa Novans' first win over MSC in nine seasons, and it came with Mount alumnus Andy Branchaud behind the Novans bench. Mount later rebounded to thump the Novans 9–3, but in between, it suffered through a nasty four-game losing streak that saw the Mounties allow twenty-eight goals in that period of time. MSC ended the season in last place, 8–14–1, as East Providence High captured both the state and New England championships.

"My first mistake was mentioning that I was influenced by Russian hockey," Shea quips. "It's amazing that it could be the same game, with sticks and pucks and ice…yet so different." Steve Shea's vision of indoctrinating a Mount team in the Russian style of hockey would come a generation later, with his daughters a part of his dream. Meanwhile, for three seasons, and for two different coaches with vastly dissimilar coaching styles, Bill Belisle toiled without complaint. Yet while the Mount varsity finished in last place, the Belisle-coached JV team completed an undefeated season.

"My father…would never criticize Mr. Tobin or Mr. Shea. He was always respectful, but from the sidelines, I could tell it was eating away at him," says John Belisle.

Fortunately, Bill Belisle had constituents lobbying on his behalf. Shortly after the conclusion of the 1974–75 season, Mount principal Brother John Hebert called an emergency meeting with the undergraduates on the team. He was considering a coaching change. Whom did they want for their next coach? John Belisle recalls:

> So we had to go into this meeting…Bear in mind, as much as I praise my father—and I still do—when I was a junior, the worst thing that could have happened to me was to have my father be head coach because I knew how strict he was, how hard he was. I knew…my brother would get it even harder from my father in terms of how hard he would be on us. And people on the outside would think he'd be easier on us. I didn't want to have any of that suspicion, and for all those reasons, no way did I want my father to be head coach my senior year. I'd waited all my life to play for Mount, and I didn't want any drama in my senior year; I just wanted to play. When the vote was cast, we did it by closing our eyes and raising our hands. When my father's name came up…all the other players on the team had seen my father coach many years and knew what a great coach he was, and they all wanted him. That was reflected in the vote because everybody raised their hand except me and my brother David. I peeked, thinking, "Please nobody have their hand up," because I didn't have my hand up. Everybody had their hand up except David, but David even raised his hand when he

*looked because he didn't want it to get back to my father that he didn't raise his hand. I didn't because I was upset. So, lo and behold, my father does become head coach, and it obviously worked out for the best. I was very scared, thinking, "My God…my father, what's he going to do to us?" As it turned out, what he ended up teaching us was about discipline, sacrifice and perseverance. We learned all those skills…and we turned the team around.*

Bill Belisle has always preached and embodied respect for self, others and team. So when the Mount administration discussed the open coaching position with him, Belisle agreed to accept it, but only with Shea's express approval. Shea gave it.

Part III

# ASCENSION INTO GREATNESS

## Chapter 6
# THE "HOUSE" THAT COACH BILL BUILT

Bill Belisle may be a man of unshakable Christian faith, but he's not one to place his faith in destiny. Still, it's hard to picture him as anything but the face of Mount Saint Charles hockey. The son of Albertine Gervais Belisle and Odias Belisle, one of the many Canadian immigrants to work in the Blackstone Valley mills, Bill Belisle grew up in Manville, Rhode Island, playing hockey on local ponds but dreaming of playing hockey in Canada. Odias Belisle, whose belief in education rivaled the Brothers of the Sacred Heart's faith in the Lord, shipped his son to Mount Saint Charles Academy, where he knew Bill would master the rudiments of writing, reading and praying. In the 1940s, the academy accepted a large number of troubled students who needed the hard-nosed direction the Brothers of the Sacred Heart provided. Bill Belisle was hardly a troubled youth; still, through the Brothers' instruction, Belisle learned lessons about self-discipline, respect, hard work and perseverance.

Despite his father's initial concern, Belisle played varsity hockey for the Mount under head coach Brother Victoric. Like the other Brothers of the Sacred Heart, Brother Victoric trained his players to push through challenges. Practices, for instance, were held even while it snowed; players were expected to shovel the snow off the surface of the outdoor ice rinks.

"It was like Canada," says Bill Belisle. "That really inspired me to push my hockey, to try to make the second line, try to make the first line."

As a junior on the 1946–47 team, Belisle and his Mounties captured the tenth state title in the program's history.

# A History of Mount Saint Charles Hockey

---

**RHODE ISLAND INTERSCHOLASTIC LEAGUE**

Kathryn A. Crowley
*Chairperson*

Richard B. Lynch
*Executive Director*

Richard R. Magarian
*Assistant Executive Director*

Bldg. #6  R.I. College Campus
600 Mt. Pleasant Avenue ♦ Providence, Rhode Island ♦ 02908-1991
Tel: (401) 272-9844 ♦ Fax: (401) 272-9838
website: www.riil.org ♦ email: info@riil.org

December 29, 2003

Mr. (Normand) Bill Belisle
372 Old River Road
Manville, RI  02838

Dear Bill,

It is with great pleasure that I write to formally inform you that you have been selected for induction into the Rhode Island Interscholastic League High School Athletic Hall of Fame.

The Class of 2004 is the second outstanding group to be inducted into the Rhode Island Interscholastic League High School Hall of Fame. Your success and accomplishments, as well as those of your fellow inductees, continue the tradition set last year of honoring exceptional people.

The Induction Banquet will be held on Wednesday, April 28, 2004 at the Quidnesset Country Club. I will contact you with more information in the near future.

Once again, congratulations on being a recipient of this honor. If you have any questions, please do not hesitate to call me.

Sincerely,

Dick

Richard B. Lynch
Executive Director

c: Hall of Fame Committee
   File

*The Rhode Island Interscholastic League does not discriminate on the basis of age, sex, race, religion, national origin, color or handicap in accordance with applicable laws and regulations.*

---

This 2003 letter from the Rhode Island Interscholastic League informed Mount Saint Charles boys hockey head coach Bill Belisle of his selection for induction into the RIIL High School Athletic Hall of Fame. *Photo courtesy of Bill Belisle.*

"Geez—I thought I had the Stanley Cup won," recalls Belisle. "That stayed with me a long time."

The following year, Mount withdrew from the RIIL for one season due to another dispute over the use of Canadian players. The Mount Varsity, as the club was known, finished the season a robust 8–1 but had no state title

Bill Belisle gives his best "master and commander" pose for what appears to be a rare promotional photo. *Photo courtesy of Bill Belisle.*

for which it could compete. "We played for nothing," remembers Bill Belisle. "We weren't going to get a championship trophy or win the states, so in a way, it wasn't rewarding. That was a disappointment: your senior year, that's your best year, you have to be part of just a regular hockey team. It was a little setback in my senior year."

After graduating from MSC, Belisle played hockey in a few amateur leagues. He served in the Korean War, achieving the rank of staff sergeant. Good with his hands and fixing things, he began to ply his trade as a mechanic. He did return to the Mount for two seasons in the mid-1950s as assistant coach to Andy Tremblay. Then, in 1974, Belisle accepted the arena manager's position at Adelard Arena. It was a move that would forever change his life and the history of MSC hockey.

Growing up in Manville, Woonsocket's neighbor, Belisle not only learned the value of community spirit—he lived it. Manville was, in many ways, an all-inclusive, self-supporting community; there was one catering business, one bowling alley (Bill Belisle was the pinsetter for years) and one cinema. Yvette Belisle's (née Beaudoin) father owned a catering business in Manville and operated it from the basement of the home in which Bill and Yvette still live. Beaudoin Catering was a hub for weddings, funerals and other gatherings. It was a hub of social interaction, and for many years, Bill Belisle was one of the waiters.

When the local little league could not support the number of kids interested in playing, Belisle founded a Manville farm league. He went door to door recruiting players, signed sponsors, organized the schedule and got his friends to coach. Soon, his league boasted six teams. Today, the league still exists. "That's how passionate he was for the town and for his kids," says Dave Belisle.

Caring for others has long been a linchpin of the Manville psyche, and volunteering was a way of life for Bill Belisle and the other townspeople. Without volunteers, there would have been no farm-league baseball or the ham-and-beans dinner or any other number of social functions. Bill Belisle served on the volunteer fire department for twenty years, and his four sons were all altar boys at Saint James Church until they were sixteen years old. (Even today, Bill Belisle attends Mass at least three mornings per week.) Every Sunday, the Belisles and their kids visited their mémère and pépère (the French translation for "grandma" and "grandpa"). "The whole town was going to see their mémères and pépères on Sunday," quips Dave. "That's how the family bonds. It's one o'clock, and we go to the car, and there's no excuses. We all went. Now, in my generation, I'm lucky if I can get all my kids to the table once or twice a year."

These strict but nurturing small-town ideals, coupled with the discipline imparted by the Brothers, helped stir in Belisle a passion for helping others and for serving Mount Saint Charles and the hockey players. So, as he prepared for the 1975–76 season, Bill Belisle "took with him a lot of tradition, a lot of pride that he wanted to instill in the program and continue."

As an assistant to Steve Shea, Belisle had silently observed numerous occasions in practice when attending fans and parents criticized Shea's efforts to implement the Russian style of hockey. When he became head coach, Belisle closed off practices to outsiders, including players' families and friends and the loyal Brothers who'd made the arena a second home. As hockey coach, Belisle lacked the authority to enforce the controversial edict.

But as arena manager, Belisle had the authority to shut the door to all but the school principal and athletic director. "You can't have twenty-five people running the team," Belisle explains.

"It became my father's team," recalls John Belisle, a senior on his father's first team. "He made it clear to parents that he was never one for parental or outside involvement. It was always about his team. He was going to coach it the best way he could and did not appreciate outside interference. When you go through those locked doors, you pretty much belong to the team."

The "No Parking" notice informs the unaware of who's in charge of both the MSC Arena and the Mount hockey team. *Author's collection.*

From day one, Bill Belisle raised the bar for the Mount hockey players. He had full confidence that his system would succeed. "I said to myself, 'If I can't reach those kids, I can't blame the parents, I can't blame the Brothers. I blame Coach Belisle. I had them all under my tutelage [as JV coach].'"

Belisle created an air of competition from the opening of tryouts; no one, not even the team captain, was automatically guaranteed a spot on the varsity. To make the Mount varsity in the early days of the Belisle reign was a feat in itself, tantamount to auditioning for a Broadway play or the television show *Fear Factor*. Tryouts ran for days, not just hours. No one was spared the wrath of Coach Belisle, not even his kids. Then, like now, Bill Belisle had no favorites.

Dave Belisle remembers the first practice under his father:

> *I was even nervous myself, saying, "Holy shit, am I going to make this team?" It was a fight out there. When people started realizing that their jobs weren't secure, we had probably one of the most heated and vibrant tryouts that I have ever been involved with. That carried on every tryout after that. People coming back said they were mentally ready and that they wanted to get in that dressing room. And I remember him [Bill Belisle] putting kids in the dressing room not all at once...it went on for five days. He only kept three lines, and he didn't want to make any mistakes.*

From that first tryout grew an annual ritual: the first guy picked (usually the best player on the team) enters the dressing room and chooses a choice stall, usually the first one, by the door. Thereafter, one by one, each player picks his spot in the varsity room until there are no spots left. There, each player will remain for the duration of the year—*if* he earns it. There are no guarantees in Coach Belisle's program.

The intensity and competitive spirit of that first tryout continued into the 1975–76 season. John Belisle was a first-line forward during his father's inaugural campaign. He recalls:

*My father did not spare anything. We'd get chewed out twice as hard as anybody and get consequences twice as hard because he wanted to make it clear that there were no favorites. He hated prima donnas. He'd knock you down in a heartbeat, so we'd get it hard on the ice, and we'd get it hard in the truck on the way home, too. The famous pickup [truck]…me and Dave got into that red pickup knowing we'd get another earful on the way home. If we were ever injured, my father made it clear when he said, "Don't be crying to your mother when you get home, either!" My mom [Yvette Belisle], being a hockey mom and wife her whole life, knew how rough a sport it could be, and that's why she never went to any games. She would stay home and pray for us because she didn't like to see her kids get hurt. Being a senior, like any other teenager wanting independence, I bumped heads with my parents, but not in any disrespectful way—that just wasn't tolerated. Did I like my dad for how hard he was on us our senior year? No. That's just being honest.*

After getting an earful from his father all season, John Belisle experienced his dad's nurturing side. When the club met for its 1975–76 postseason banquet, Coach Bill named three team MVPs. The last name he announced was John Belisle. "It was nice that my father recognized me in that way," recalls John. "He wasn't one to give a lot of verbal praise and high fives. The way he did it, he gave the last MVP to me. When my name came up, I was like, 'What?' It was totally unexpected."

Mount finished its first season under Bill Belisle 29–8–1, losing in the state semifinals. For junior Dave Belisle, it was probably the "longest year of my life." "I was very immature, but I thought he was single-handedly picking me out," says Dave. "But what I didn't realize was that I came in with some concept that it was going to be difficult, and he treated me just like anybody else that wasn't trying as hard or wasn't listening. I was a good player, but I could have been a much better player my junior year if I had played up to his expectations. I thought it was personal. We got into a lot of battles."

A year later, a more mature senior captain Dave Belisle did play up to his father's expectations. It was his turn to perform in his celebrated senior season. Something clicked; his father's lessons took root. The 1976–77 campaign was bittersweet for both Dave Belisle and the Mounties. MSC improved to 33–4 but lost in three games to defending champ LaSalle in the state finals. Coming so close to winning a state title but failing haunted Dave Belisle for years to come. "For a long period, it really did. I think it bothered me so much that I wanted to come back and win and win and win. It was always in the back of my mind. And then it didn't bother me when we lost [The Streak]."

Mount entered the 1977–78 season loaded with talent and bent on knocking off LaSalle. By now, Belisle's coaching system was paying significant dividends, thanks in large part to practices that made actual games seem like two hours of free skating.

Ed Lee, an all-star forward at Mount and future NHL draft pick, played on the 1978 and 1979 teams. He remembers how tough the practices were but how they helped him in years to come:

> *He* [Bill Belisle] *got into a culture in that rink where he could be in locker room and he would leave a puck on the ice. The lights were dim, and we'd go out and skate around. If we weren't on the ice by a certain time—Boom! your bags were packed. He might throw you right off the team. There were times when he might have been rushing around the locker room to get out there…we were so trained militarily that we would start sprinting around in circles to the right. Suddenly he'd blow his whistle twice, and that meant stop and go the other way—slowly. He'd blow the whistle again, and you'd pick it up. Nobody touched the puck. If you ever touched the puck he left out there on purpose to see…if we would start screwing around—forget about it. We would do sprints and sprints and sprints until it was brutal. That was what he brought his first few years. When we got him, he was a rattlesnake. I was a tough punk from Providence, and I wouldn't even make eye contact with him. Practices were a death walk, and games were so easy and fun because you were so prepared.*

Belisle was a master at spotting even the slightest flaw in a player's game. Then, without hesitation, he'd do whatever it took to correct that weakness.

For instance, during one practice, Belisle summoned Lee to center ice. He pointed to the player's skates, his stance. Your first step is wrong, he told Lee.

"My two skates were too close to each other. He made me move one skate one inch from the other, and it was like, 'You have to be kidding me,'" says Lee.

He wasn't. Belisle, whose power-skating clinics would become legendary, recognized that a proper skating technique begins with the first step, the key to quickness.

Lee recalls one practice when forward Freddie Barker developed problems with his skates. Belisle stopped the practice and, with Barker prone on the ice, unlaced the player's skates. He then carried Barker's skates into the lobby and had the blades sharpened. Belisle returned to the ice, put the skates back on Barker's feet and laced them up.

"He wouldn't have him falling down out there," chuckles Lee.

Another time, Belisle made Dan Potter, one of the team's best players, do wind sprints of a different kind.

"The puck ended up in the stands," recalls Lee, "and Coach Belisle sends Potter into the stands with his skates on. He made him, for the hour and a half or so left in practice, go against the boards where the penalty box is. He made him sprint from blue line to blue line, at center ice, right against the boards... Every time we looked over, Potter was still going—barely, but still going. That's why parents weren't allowed in practice. That's why if there was a problem between two players in the corner of the ice, he would put them at center ice and let them have a fight."

If you're a Mount alumnus or longtime fan, you've likely heard at least one of the many legendary stories—some as tall as a Mark Twain story, others brutally honest—culled from the scores of Belisle-run practices. Each drill, no matter how seemingly illogical or brutal, was designed to help the players to improve. John Belisle recalls:

> *From Mount hockey, I got more than one thing. The most important thing that stands out was that my father was big on "Mount Pride." Mount always had that high standard, and as kids growing up, we always wanted to be a part of that* [and] *continue the tradition. When my father came, he let you know that when you came into that rink, there was no more individual. There was no more I; there was just the team and giving 100 percent for your team, and when you did that, you walked away with a lot of satisfaction—not so much what you accomplished as an individual but as part of a team, part of a family. You knew you had given all you had for that family, and you felt great about leaving. With that you learn*

## Ascension into Greatness

History! The state champion Mounties completed the 1978–79 campaign a perfect 30–0 and ranked second in the nation. Here, Coach Bill Belisle christens senior captain and all-state forward Pat Manocchia with a bit of the "bubbly." *Photo courtesy of Bill Belisle.*

> *self-discipline, sacrifice, stamina, perseverance…all those things that go along with being successful at any sport. My father taught us everything, especially discipline, and unfortunately, I think that's lacking these days.*

For nearly forty years, the Belisles—Bill and Dave—have provided the discipline "these kids need," says Dave Belisle. "It works…it really does work."

The discipline and hard work paid off in 1977–78. Mount avenged its loss to LaSalle in the previous season's finals by beating the Rams to win the championship. In going 35–1 that year, Mount also captured the New England title.

The Streak had been born. Soon, winning was accompanied by the pressure of maintaining the skein of Rhode Island state titles. Throughout the twenty-six-season streak, Dave Belisle reminded his players—especially the seniors—to keep things in perspective. This was only a game, after all.

"I kept preaching to the kids to go out and enjoy the moment," says Dave Belisle. He continues:

*Once you start to think about what the results would be and how you're going to handle it as the game goes on, you're done. Shift by shift... everything with my father was shift by shift, and now I understand why. When you look ahead or revert back, you are in trouble. Just think about what you're supposed to do in that shift. Move the puck and communicate; don't harp on the last shift. You listen to my tutelage and go out there. The people who sulk or worry about it don't perform well. Then you have the person who keeps checking the clock...the good ones are never checking the clock; they hop off, and they're ready to get back on. A little breather and a little squirt of the water, and they're ready to go. Those are the guys that are going to win you those championships.*

Was Bill Belisle ever nervous during the championship games of The Streak? "No. I was still doing the same things. I know what to do; hockey's a simple game. Play the way I want you to play—Mount Pride, and that's it."

For years, Coach Bill has run the team practices while Coach Dave manages the team during the games. While his father may be calm and collected during

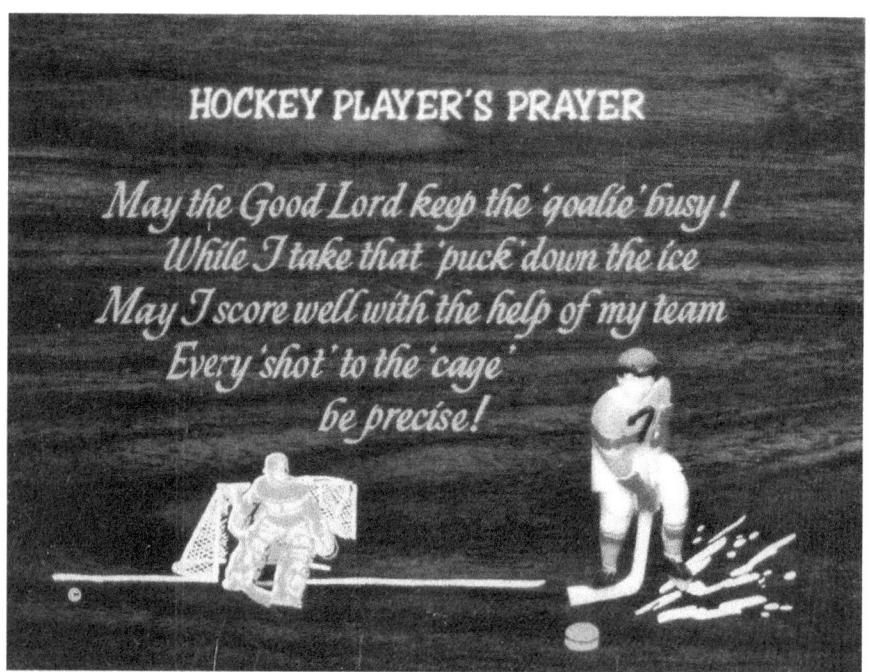

The maxim for a hockey player. *Photo courtesy of Bill Belisle.*

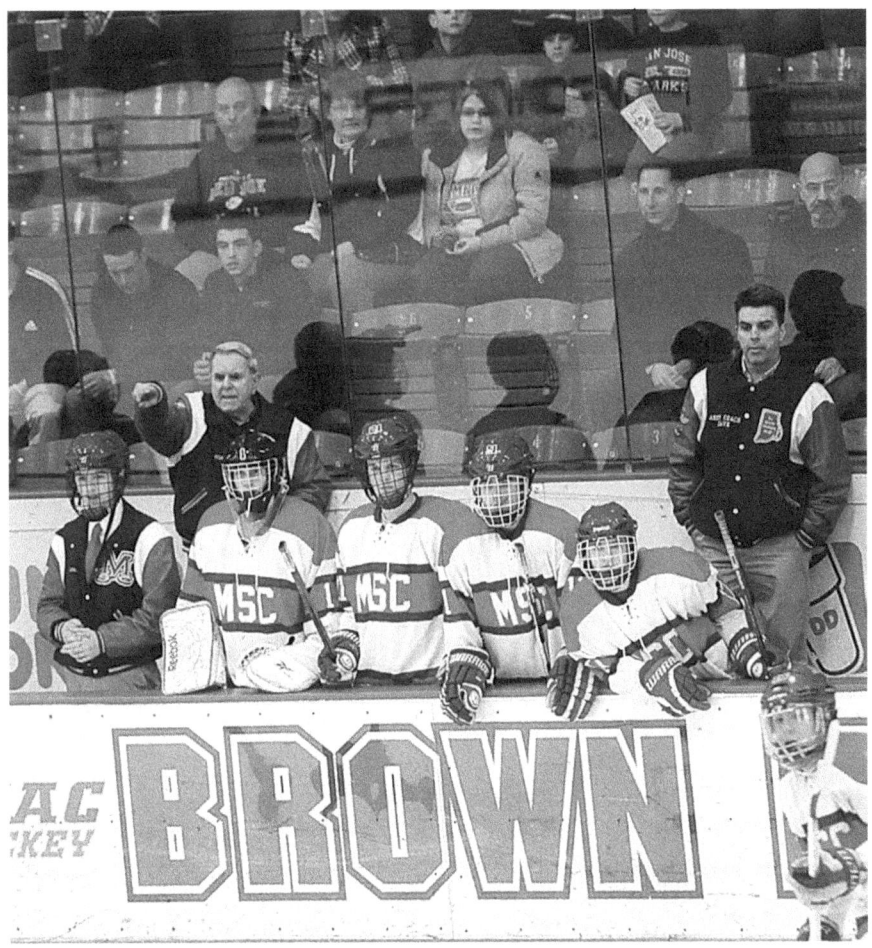

Co-coach Bill Belisle shouts instructions to his players during Game 1 of the 2013 state championship playoffs. *Photo courtesy of Ernest Brown.*

big games, Dave Belisle is a cauldron of excitement. "Before the games, I'm jacked up. I have to be as intense during the games as he is during practice," says Dave. "I've got to make sure they believe I am on the ice with them. I'm pushing the right buttons because I see what they are doing with him in practice. He's correcting it in practice, and I get to take all that he has corrected and all that tutelage, and I've got to play the right guys at the right time. It's on me. That's the responsibility he's given me all these years."

In this way, two Belisle minds have melded into one mind. And this one mind, for twenty-six straight seasons, was Rhode Island's best.

Chapter 7

# STREAKING THROUGH THE STREAK: HIGHLIGHTS OF THE TWENTY-SIX CONSECUTIVE MOUNT SAINT CHARLES STATE CHAMPIONSHIPS

1977–78: The series that kicked off The Streak saw a determined Mount Saint Charles (35–1) avenge its 1976–77 title-series loss to LaSalle in vengeful fashion. The Mount opened the title series by slamming the Rams 8–2. LaSalle, champions of two consecutive titles, handed MSC its only loss of the season in Game 2, defeating the Mount 2–1. But the Mounties ramped up their offense and sealed their first title in twenty years by toppling the Rams 7–1 to take the 1977–78 championship. MSC went on to win the New England championship, as well. The Mounties placed three players on the all-state team: Mike Gouin, Jim Colucci and Dave Guevremont.

1978–79: Mount's second straight state title in the 1970s was scored by arguably the most talented team in MSC school history. The '78–'79 Mounties recorded a perfect 30–0 record while beating LaSalle for the second straight season, 5–2 and 9–2. In the series clincher, Pat Manocchia, John Viveiros and Ed Lee each scored twice for MSC. Goalie Barry McColgan earned the win but deferred praise to his teammates: "With this team in front of me, how could I lose?" he told the *Woonsocket Call*. "That's why I never worried; we have a great, great team." Manocchia, Dan Potter and Ken Fargnoli were named to the all-state team.

1979–80: The Mounties (29–0) completed their second consecutive undefeated/untied season and were named National Champions for the first of ten consecutive seasons when they swept East Providence. Game 1 was a breeze for MSC, which won 9–3. Game 2 also went to the Mounties, 4–3, with freshman and future number-one-overall NHL draft pick Brian Lawton setting up future Olympian Paul Guay for a pair of goals.

1980–81: Between 1981 and 1988, Mount and Bishop Hendricken clashed in the state finals seven times. Their first meeting, 1980–81, set the stage for a long and intense rivalry. MSC took the inaugural championship series, 5–3, 5–2, for its fourth straight title. Mount Saint Charles concluded the season at 31–0–1, the tie coming against Hendricken (2–2) in the second game of the championship series. Mike Hodson and Paul Guay, now a longtime Mount assistant, were named to the all-state team.

1981–82: This season was another one for the record book. Mount saw its one-hundred-game unbeaten streak ended by Burrillville in the Call Country Classic. No worries. The Mounties (30–2) chalked up their fifth straight state title, sweeping Hendricken 6–3 and 6–2. Doug Petrarca and Brian Lawton earned all-state honors.

1982–83: Mount's (31–1–1) sixth straight state title, a three-game nod over Hendricken (6–1, 3–4, 4–1), is remembered as much for Bill Belisle's courage as for the plaque the team garnered. On February 21, 1983, Belisle suffered a near-fatal skull fracture when he fell during practice. For days, the Mount patriarch lingered in a coma, clinging jealously to life itself. So critical was Belisle's condition that a Catholic priest was summoned to perform last rites. Belisle survived the fall, but it took him nearly two years to recover fully. Coach Bill did return for the 1983–84 season, arguably the most personally challenging of his coaching career.

In 1983, MSC placed four members on the all-state team: Brian Lawton, Greg Pratt, Jay Octeau and Alan Perry. Lawton also entered the Mount history books when he became the first American chosen number one overall when Minnesota selected him first in the 1982–83 draft. Two others Mounties from the 1982–83 team were selected in the NHL draft: Tom McComb (sixth round, Minnesota) and Jay Octeau (ninth round, New Jersey).

"We had an employee at the rink who used to open the door for Brian [Lawton] at two or three in the morning," remembers Bill Belisle. "I said, 'Don't worry, let him practice all by himself.'"

Coaches Dave and Bill Belisle are pictured with former Mountie Brian Lawton. In 1983, Lawton became the first American-born player selected first overall in the NHL draft. Lawton recorded 266 career points in 483 NHL games. *Photo courtesy of Bill Belisle.*

1983–84: Mount (24–2–2) coasted past Cranston East, 10–4 and 7–1, to earn its seventh straight Rhode Island title. For the season, MSC outscored its opposition 186–39. Mike Morrison and Alan Perry were named to the all-state team. Perry, who left the Mount after his junior year, enjoyed a successful minor-league hockey career, especially in the International Hockey League. "Alan Perry—the way he'd come out and challenge the shooter..." says Bill Belisle. "I'd yell, 'Alan, stay in your net every once in a while!' 'Okay, Okay,' he'd say. Oh, my goodness!" Dave Belisle adds, "He was the best high school goalie we ever had. During high school, he was the guy who stoned those Hendricken teams."

1984–85: With Bill Belisle finally returning to form, MSC (27–1) banged past Bishop Hendricken, 2–1 and 5–0. MSC finished the season 27–1, allowing a mere thirty goals all year. Jeff Cournoyer, Chris Cambio, Matt Merten and future University of Maine star Dave Capuano were named to the all-state squad.

## Ascension into Greatness

1985–86: The Mounties (27–2) compensated for a subpar performance in their Game 2 loss (6–2) to take Game 3, 6–2, and the 1985–86 title in three games over Bishop Hendricken. MSC had taken the opener, 4–3, only to see the Hawks storm back in Game 2. Behind the offensive explosion led by all-staters Dave Capuano and Sean Boudreault and the sterling defense of Dennis Cesana, the "Good Ship Mount Saint Charles" sailed to its ninth straight title. On the season, Mount outscored its opposition 257–47. Capuano, Matt Merten and Boudreault were all selected in the 1985–86 NHL draft.

1986–87: This year provided a rags-to-riches story as powerful Bishop Hendricken was "Snowed" under by the future GM of the New York Islanders, Garth Snow. The Mounties (23–5–1) dropped the opener, 2–1, but rallied to win the second game, 5–3, and the series-clincher, 3–2. The series marked Don Armstrong's finale as Hawks' head coach. Forward Steve DiMaio, Snow and Keith E. Carney were named to the all-state team. Defenseman Mathieu Schneider, the first Mount star to leave the program early to play junior hockey, was selected by Montreal in the third round of the 1986–87 draft. Snow was a sixth-round pick of the Quebec Nordiques, while goalie Marc Felicio was an eleventh-round pick of the North Stars.

1987–88: Co-champs? No way, said the determined 24–4–3 Mounties. The best-of-three championship series climaxed in five historic battles as Hawks fans descended from Heaven to Hell with fourteen seconds left in The Streak. Mount sent two defensemen to the all-state team: Keith E. Carney and Jeff Robison. Carney, a fourth-round draft pick of the Calgary Flames, went on to star at the University of Maine before enjoying a solid career in the NHL. Robison, meanwhile, was selected in the fifth round of the 1987–88 draft by the Los Angeles Kings.

1988–89: The last of the great Mounties clubs of The Streak era, MSC (25–2–2) finished first in the nation for the tenth and final time by sweeping La Salle, 4–0 and 9–2. MSC placed five players on the all-state team: forwards Derek Chauvette, Brian Ridolfi and Brian Jefferies and defensemen Keith P. Carney (fifth-round draft pick, Toronto) and Brendan Whittet. Chauvette and Whittet went on to star at Brown University, where Whittet now coaches. Ridolfi and Jefferies went on to team with former Hendricken star Rob Gaudreau at Providence College.

1989–90: Senior Jon Jacques emerged as one of the best forwards in the state as he led MSC to a sweep (6–1, 4–2) of LaSalle and earning Mount its thirteenth straight state title. Jacques and defenseman Dean Capuano were named to the all-state team for the Mounties, who finished 23–5–1. MSC, for the first time since the 1978–79 season, was not ranked first in the country (third).

1990–91: During the Mounties' twenty-six-year streak of consecutive state titles, few clubs came as close to surrendering the championship as the 1990–91 club. MSC was up 4–0 in Game 1 of its title series with LaSalle when the roof caved in. The deeper, more talented Rams rallied to topple MSC 6–5 and headed into Game 2 favored to win their first title since 1977. However, MSC (21–7–2) rallied in double overtime to win 3–2 in Game 2. The Mount managed to overcome the heroics of LaSalle's all-state goalie Bob Ronzio to capture the deciding game 4–3. Junior forward Chris Murphy and junior defenseman Dennis Sousa earned all-state honors.

1991–92: MSC (28–1) made it a clean sweep of Bishop Hendricken, taking the 1991–92 state title, Mount's fifteenth straight, by scores of 6–0 and 4–2. Four Mounties made the all-state team: defensemen Jon Pirrong and Dennis Sousa and forwards Chris Murphy and Dan Lavergne. For Lavergne, playing at Mount provided him with the work ethic and self-confidence to succeed both on and off the ice. Today, he is the president and a minority owner of the Odessa (Texas) Jackalopes of the North American Hockey League. "I think Bill Belisle turned me into a man," says Lavergne. "I grew up without a father, and Bill Belisle prepared me for life's challenges. Life's a hard roller coaster. That man and Dave [Belisle] prepared me for manhood. They teach you about teamwork and work ethic and never give up. I was a shy kid, and I was intimidated at first for a few years. My junior year, I was first-team all-state and led the league in scoring. Chris Murphy brought me under his wing. Was it fun? Definitely. But there was also pressure. Anything you do in life that is on a big stage, you are going to have expectations, but you gotta make it fun. Mount is an amazing school, first and foremost. I learned more about myself in six years at Mount than at any other time in my life."

1992–93: The 1992–93 Mounties boasted one of their deepest teams in years, with three forwards—Dan Lavergne, Frank Fede and Adam Gilbert—earning all-state honors. With three excellent forward lines and five skilled rearguards, MSC blew past LaSalle in the finals, 5–3 and 10–1, to finish the

## Ascension into Greatness

As a junior on the 1992 MSC squad, Dan Lavergne (white jersey, #19) led the league in scoring as MSC swept Bishop Hendricken to win the state title. A year later, the senior forward and two-time all-state selection led the Mounties to a two-game sweep of LaSalle in the 1993 championship series. Today, Lavergne is the president and a minority owner of the Odessa (Texas) Jackalopes of the North American Hockey League. *Photo courtesy of the author.*

year 27–1–1. The club featured a blossoming Mount star and a future U.S. Olympian and veteran of ten NHL seasons in defenseman Bryan Berard. The first player chosen in the 1994–95 NHL draft, Berard returned from a serious eye injury in 2000 to play with a special contact lens that improved his damaged vision to the league minimum of 20/400. As a sophomore at Mount, Berard was already the best defenseman in the state. "He was Woonsocket-city tough," says Dave Belisle. "He had to fight for everything growing up; his father was a simple mechanic, and his best buddy was [goalie Brian] Boucher. They spent every hour competing together; they pushed each other. It was a matter of survival."

Meanwhile, senior forward Matt Grieve parlayed his Mount experience and education into the coaching ranks. As the head coach at Mount Hope High School, Grieve led his Huskies to a 2010 Division III title. "It was amazing; you have a lot of pressure as a player, but to be coach and everything going on, it was unbelievable," says Grieve. "I had great kids…

# A History of Mount Saint Charles Hockey

Adam Gilbert was an all-state forward and Mount captain during the 1992–93 season. *Photo courtesy of the author.*

Mount forward Ryan Murphy (white shirt) played two seasons for MSC before taking his stick and game to the prep hockey ranks. *Photo courtesy of the author.*

## Ascension into Greatness

Former Mount greats often reconnect at Mount Saint Charles Arena to celebrate their high school careers. *From left to right*: Coach Dave Belisle, longtime team physician Dr. Jean Guay, Paul Guay, Jeff Jillson, Brian Boucher, Garth Snow, Mathieu Schneider and Coach Bill Belisle. *Photo courtesy of Bill Belisle.*

we had lost to them [runner-up Rogers High] twice in the regular season. During the championships, we had two good games and won. It was just a lot of fun. I try to make Mount Hope Pride in my players."

1993–94: Led by all-state defenseman Dan Zaluski and forward Chris Leclair, the Mounties (24–2–1) breezed to their national record–setting seventeenth straight state title. MSC eclipsed Notre Dame High's (Berlin, New Hampshire) record of sixteen straight titles by topping Bishop Hendricken 8–1 and 8–4 after also sweeping LaSalle in the semifinals. Future NHL first-round pick and veteran NHL goalie Brian Boucher (another Woonsocket native) allowed six goals in four playoff games.

"It's special," Bill Belisle told the *Woonsocket Call* after the series-clinching win. "When we won four or five or six in a row, you'd never think about something like this. But when we won thirteen or fourteen in a row, I started thinking about it. I'd be a hypocrite if I said I didn't."

# A History of Mount Saint Charles Hockey

Frank Fede (left, #14) joins in the celebration of a Mount goal. Fede was an all-state forward as a senior and enjoyed a fine playing career for the Army Black Knights men's ice hockey team. *Author's collection.*

1994–95: Mount's eighteenth straight title did not come easily. Goalie Brian Oliver backboned the defense and Matt Kohansky and Chris Leclair the offense as Mount (21–6–1) slipped past Bishop Hendricken in three games. Led by stars Jason Ialongo and Jay Shaw, the Hawks took Game 1, 2–1. Mount, however, rallied to win the next two contests, 2–0 and 3–1.

1995–96: In the December 1995 edition of *Hockey Digest*, Bill Belisle predicted the following: "I think this is the year that I expect to be knocked off the ladder. But I keep looking at the (Adelard Arena) wall (festooned with banners of Mount championships), and I tell myself I have to keep climbing up the ladder. If I say eighteen (straight titles) is enough, I've had it."

Not in 1996. The Mounties (23–2–1) made it nineteen in a row by topping Toll Gate in three games. This series, however, belonged to future U.S. Olympic goalie Sara DeCosta. The all-state netminder defied reason and gravity in nearly leading the Titans to the upset. She led all playoff goalies with 169 saves.

## Ascension into Greatness

A three-time Rhode Island all-state defenseman, Jeff Jillson led the Mounties to four state titles. He was the fourteenth overall pick in the first round of the 1999 NHL Draft (San Jose Sharks). Jillson went on to star at the University of Michigan under legendary coach Red Berenson. *Photo courtesy of Bill Belisle.*

Her team, meanwhile, overcame a 4–3 overtime loss in Game 1. In Game 2, DeCosta became the first goalie in eighteen years to record a shutout (3–0) of the Mounties in a title game. Mount rallied behind Matt Kohansky and Brian Glaude to win the rubber match 5–1. Matt Kohansky, Brian Glaude, Kevin Beauregard and Jeff Jillson were named to the all-state team.

1996–97: The Mounties (23–4–1) easily dispatched Toll Gate to take the 1996–97 title, their twentieth straight. MSC followed a 5–2 romp in Game 1 with a 10–1 rout of the Titans in the finale. Gil Lefort, who came into his own in his senior season, was named series MVP. Frank Maniglia, Charlie Ridolf and future University of Michigan star Jeff Jillson were named to the all-state team.

1997–98: Star defenseman and future NHL pick Jeff Jillson (four goals and five assists in five playoff games) was named series MVP as MSC (21–7–1) made it twenty-one straight, beating Hendricken 2–1 in overtime in Game 1 and 5–0 in Game 2. Sophomore Chris Snizek and Jillson earned all-state honors.

# A History of Mount Saint Charles Hockey

1998–99: After losing 6–1 to Hendricken in the opening game, Mount's streak of twenty-one straight titles looked tenuous. However, with a roster loaded with talented sophomore forwards, MSC (22–8–2) turned its game around and hammered the Hawks 8–1 to send the series to a third and deciding game. MSC continued its inspired play and made it twenty-two titles in a row with a 4–1 triumph of the Hawks in the rubber match. Senior forwards Matt Roy and Sean Jackson provided the leadership, sophomore star Chris Chaput chipped in the goals and netminder Pete Capizzo shut the door on the Hawks in Games 2 and 3.

1999–2000: Mount's (27–4–1) twenty-third consecutive state title came in series of "twos." They needed two games to slide past a stubborn LaSalle Academy team (4–2, 2–1); two star junior forwards, Justin Laverdiere and Chris Chaput; and two very good goalies, Pete Capizzo and Anthony Ciresi III.

2000–01: The following season featured "Goalies Gone Wild." LaSalle goalie Jim Merola almost single-handedly kick-saved the Rams to what would have been their first state title since 1976–77. In eight playoff games, the senior netminder and championship series MVP recorded 231 saves. In Game 1 of the finals, he led the Maroon to a stunning 2–1 victory over MSC. Then, in Game 2, Merola and his club entered overtime one goal away from a state title. However, senior forward Justin Laverdiere rallied the Mounties to a 3–2 win by beating Merola with a quick wrist shot in overtime. MSC (28–3–1) pulled away to take Game 3, 6–3.

MSC, meanwhile, rotated talented goalies Ryan Hatch and Anthony Ciresi III. Hatch dropped the opener, but Ciresi III won Game 2. Coaches Bill and Dave Belisle went with Hatch in the rubber match, and he did not disappoint.

As tense as the netminders were, few were as nervous as former Mount goalie and assistant coach Tony Ciresi, father of Anthony Ciresi III. "There is no contest!" says Ciresi, who backboned Mount to the 1972 title and followed with ten more state titles as a Mount assistant from 1980 to 1990. "Watching my son in goal with the ridiculous pressure of the 'winning streak' was beyond anything I had experienced at any level. Those kids (and parents) had zero fun. It wasn't a case of, 'Yippee, we won!' It was, 'Thank God we didn't lose.' My heart goes out to the kids that were the first to lose. That streak was absurd…the entire format favored MSC…adding three minutes to each period and two out of three [games] instead of winners/losers brackets like everywhere else. Jeff Robison and Garth Snow were the main culprits in keeping that streak alive."

# Ascension into Greatness

Members of the 2001–02 Mount club celebrate the program's twenty-fifth consecutive state title. Leading the way was senior captain and all-state forward Matt Roy (#19). *Photo courtesy of Bill Belisle.*

Corey Goglia, pictured here preparing for a faceoff, led Mount to state titles in 2002 and 2003. He was an all-state selection both years and one of the state's premier scorers. *Photo courtesy of Bill Belisle.*

*Left*: Kick save and a beauty! Ryan Hatch extends himself to shunt aside an opposing shot. Hatch was an all-state selection in 2002. *Photo courtesy of Bill Belisle.*

*Below*: Seniors Patrick Ciummo (left) and Nathan Perreault (right) celebrate the Mount program's twenty-sixth consecutive Rhode Island high school hockey state championship in 2003. *Photo courtesy of Bill Belisle.*

2001–02: Mount's great offensive depth, led by Corey Goglia, and strong goaltending from Ryan Hatch proved too much for LaSalle in 2001–02. Mount methodically swept aside the Rams, 6–1 and 6–2, to make it twenty-five straight championships. Matt Roy, Stephen Snizek, Corey Goglia and Ryan Hatch made the all-state team for MSC, which finished the year 25–4.

2002–03: Perhaps a harbinger of the following season, the Mounties struggled to win their twenty-sixth straight state title. LaSalle Academy

Mount forward Brendan Shea battles for possession during the faceoff of a game in the 2002–03 season. *Photo courtesy of Bill Belisle.*

took Game 1 of the 2002–03 title series, 3–2, behind a stellar goaltending performance from Chris Rossi. MSC (26–3–1) rallied for the championship, however, taking Game 2, 3–1, and Game 3, 5–3. Corey Goglia was named series MVP.

Part IV

# GREAT GAMES, GREAT SERIES, GREAT MOMENTS

## Chapter 8
# "THE FIRST": THE STREAK BEGINS WITH THE 1978 STATE CHAMPIONSHIP

The final horn had sounded, and the celebration was at a fever pitch when Mount Saint Charles forward Jim Colucci declared to reporters, "We were the best team in the state all season long, and we sure proved it tonight." His Mounties had just vanquished longtime rival LaSalle Academy 7–1 in the deciding game of the 1978 state finals before a jubilant crowd at Adelard Arena. The win gave MSC its first state title since 1947, and it capped one of the most dominating seasons in the history of the storied program. Only a 2–1 loss to the Maroon in Game 2 of the three-game championship series prevented the Mount from recording a perfect season. Still, MSC concluded the 1977–78 campaign with a 35–1 record; the fifty-seven-shot performance in Game 3 erased the lingering disappointment of the previous season's three-game loss to the Rams in the finals.

Little did anyone know that this dominating season would mark the beginning of what would become the longest state hockey title-winning streak in high school history.

Head coach Bill Belisle told the *Woonsocket Call* that after the 2–1 loss in Game 2, it was "just a matter of time before we opened things up."

They did so in what would become true Mount Style: unflagging speed and discipline, superior checking and contribution from the team stars.

After a scoreless first period, the Mount came out storming in the middle stanza of Game 3. By the six-minute mark, the Mounties had peppered LaSalle goalie Tracy McCann (thirty-three saves to win Game 2) with sixteen shots. They converted three of those into goals, one each by Mike

Samborsky, Dan Potter and Pat Manocchia. The Rams jumped back into the contest when Dave Harrington beat Mount goalie Dave Guevremont to make it 3–1. But Mike Gouin's tally sent the teams to the locker room with Mount up 4–1.

The onslaught continued in a third period that punctuated Mount's conviction to slam the door on a Rams' championship three-peat. Bob Carignan netted two of the final three goals to give MSC what would become known as "The First": state title number one of twenty-six consecutive.

## Chapter 9
# THE FOURTEEN-SECOND MIRACLE

For one week in March 1988, Mount Saint Charles and Bishop Hendricken waged war in what remains the most grueling, exhausting (for fans and players alike) and engaging title bout in Rhode Island high school hockey history. Officially, MSC reeled in its eleventh straight state title in three games, rallying from a 7–6 loss in Game 1 to beat the Hawks 5–0 and 5–1 in "Games 2 and 3."

However, those official statistics are mere illusion. The Hawks and Mounties battled through an additional two double-overtime ties that were ruled non-games. Those two games, a 4–4 tie in "Game 3" and 2–2 tie in "Game 4" left fans of both teams breathless, some of the best players in the state vanquished and the headline of the lead sports story of the March 10, 1988 *Woonsocket Call* musing wistfully, "Will Mount-Hendricken Series Ever End?"

Were one of the combatants anyone but MSC, the series likely would have ended in the fourth contest, with Hendricken winning 2–1 and capturing its first state title. Instead, Hendricken fans came within fourteen seconds of winning high school hockey's version of the lottery, only to have yet another hero in Mount hockey lore step to the forefront.

Senior defenseman and co-captain Jeff Robison was known more as an ice general than a deft scorer. But with the season on the line and the Mount's ten-year skein of state titles hanging in the balance, Robison picked the right time to utilize his offensive skills and ice vision.

The scene: With thirty seconds left in regulation, Hendricken fans were on their feet screaming their support deliriously. So close were they to celebrating the defeat of the Mighty Mount…so close. On the opposite side of Meehan Auditorium, the Mount faithful also stood—breathlessly exhorting their team to pull off a miracle and score the game-tying goal.

Time continued to tick away on The Streak. From the Mount bench, assistant coach Dave Belisle exhorted his players to push onward, to take things shift by shift. A second on the Mount Saint Charles time clock was an eternity to the opposition, for head coach Bill Belisle drummed into the heads and souls of every player: "You battle until the end."

And battle they did—for a loose puck behind the Hendricken net. As Hawks goalie Dave Berard slid to his right post to guard against a potential Mount wraparound, Robison cruised into the high slot from his blue-line position. When the puck squirted in his direction, Robison's hockey instincts took over, and he snapped off a quick wrist shot targeted for the far corner of the net. With adequate time and the presence to come out of his cage, cut down the angle and square himself to the shooter, Berard may have stopped Robison's shot. Berard, however, was unable to reposition himself in time to fend off Robison's shot, which rippled the twines and sent the MSC faithful and players into a state of pandemonium. The number fourteen glowed brightly in the "seconds" column of the time clock. The Hendricken fans, meanwhile, so insanely close to celebrating the biggest win the program's history, stood in silent despair.

With the game knotted at two, the teams battled through two scoreless overtimes. This time, Mount freshman goalie Pat Scetta, who entered the contest with just five games of varsity experience, came up big in overtime. With one minute and forty seconds left in the second extra period, Scetta stoned Rob Gaudreau—the best two-way player in the state—on a breakaway. The rest, as they say, went into the record books—or, to be accurate, *did not* go into the record books. As it had for the previous game's 4–4 tie, the league declared the 2–2 tie a "non-game." League officials also ruled that co-champions would be declared should the fifth game end in an overtime tie. Some twenty-four years later, Robison looks back on the game:

> *Fourteen seconds—it's nice to think back on it. It was great pressure and then the relief. The puck was coming out in front, and I kind of knew where I was, so I fired quick before Berard could get set—and that's all it was. It was more relief than happiness. I never felt like a hero; I was just part of the team. When I was on the team and playing…that was all that mattered. The* [Mount] *jacket—the varsity coat—was a sense of pride. It was so competitive to be on the team. All Coach Belisle preached*

*was mental toughness every day in practice—every second, every moment of every practice. If you were not practicing tough, at your top level, you wouldn't play. Looking back, it was perseverance; when things are down, you find a way to turn them around. You can take so many things from him.*

Because of or despite Robison's efforts, the deciding game remained, forty-eight hours later. Would the Hawks rally after the disheartening tie?

Robison had no doubt that they would.

"They were very high-explosive talents," says Robison. "They were really good and had one of the top talents [Rob Gaudreau] ever in high school hockey. I don't feel we ever let down in Game 1; we never let down against Hendricken because the tide could turn so quick."

Game 5 was virtually all MSC.

"By the fifth game, I was pretty much fried," recalls Gaudreau, who played on the team's first line and quarterbacked the power play. "Their depth got to us—they kept grinding it out. Mount had great talent and a go-through-the-wall mentality. We did, too, but they had more depth, and

An exhausted Pat Scetta, MSC goalie, along with teammates Keith P. Carney (sitting), Keith E. Carney (#6), Jeff Robison (#14) and Brendan Whittet (#4), collect themselves for overtime during the Mounties' epic 1988 "five-game" war with Bishop Hendricken. *Photo courtesy of Mount Saint Charles.*

their third line and defensemen…the Belisles wound them up, and that's what they do."

Junior forward Derek Chauvette led the Mount attack with two goals and an assist, while freshman goalie Pat Scetta shared series MVP honors with Hawks' goalie Dave Berard. Ironically, Game 5 was Scetta's sixth and final game in a Mount uniform; the Mount netter left the program after the school year.

Weeks later, when the national hockey rankings were announced, Mount was number one in the country for the ninth straight time. Hendricken was fifth. Were it not for Jeff Robison's goal in Game 4, Hendricken likely would have been not only the state's best team but also the nation's.

Today, the memory of the "Fourteen-Second Miracle" remains vivid for Chauvette, who assisted on Robison's historic goal and went on to star at Brown University:

> *No one panicked. Looking back…it was just part of the streak and mystique Coach Belisle created in the program. We had practiced that—bounces are a part of game. This is where Mount separates itself physically. For us, the hardest thing we did at Mount was the practices. They were tremendous; they always had a theme and purpose. We were so prepared for everything that came at us. Bill Belisle and Tony Ciresi had us so well conditioned. With Bill Belisle, you have to be mentally tough. I don't remember feeling any stress; I was very confident in our preparation. With the style of Bill Belisle…whether you were the best player or the twentieth guy, there were no days off. You could go from the first line to the second line in a hurry. Motivation replaced stress.*

## Chapter 10
# HAWKS SNOWED UNDER

With eighteen seconds remaining in the third and deciding game of the 1987 state hockey tournament, Bishop Hendricken head coach Don Armstrong felt the icy hand of reality clutch his throat. "The puck was cleared into the neutral zone, and I looked up at the clock, and there were eighteen seconds left," Armstrong recalls. "I was like, 'I don't believe that we're going to lose this game! It's unbelievable how we outplayed them!'"

To many hockey fans, the 1986–87 championship series will be remembered as the series Mount goalie Garth Snow single-handedly won. Snow repeatedly came up big in a third period in which the Hawks practically rented the Mount zone. Time and time again, Snow shut the door on the Hawks' explosive offense as the undermanned Mounties survived to win Game 3, 3–2, and captured their tenth straight state title.

"Garth Snow stonewalled us," recalls Armstrong, who retired from coaching at Hendricken after the 1987 season.

Snow, however, begs to differ, saying, "*We* won the game."

On paper, Mount probably should not have won a single game, much less the best-of-three series. The Hawks had the better talent, including the premier first line in the state—Rob Gaudreau, Steven King and David Emma—and the best player in the state in Emma. The Hawks had won the Met A regular-season title, highlighted by an 8–1 thrashing of the Mounties at Adelard Arena. Mount, meanwhile, was playing without its best forward, Mike Lacroix, who'd suffered a head injury in December and was lost for the rest of the season. At the helm stood Snow, who'd become the team's starter for his senior season.

Somehow, Mount rallied from a 2–1 opening-game loss to top the Hawks 5–3 in Game 2. Head coach Bill Belisle called the title win a matter of adhering to the "Mount Style." His players, however, knew there was more to winning than merely following the coach's game plan.

"In that locker room, we had players who cared greatly in a way similar to what we experienced at the University of Maine," Snow recalls. "Dave Duhamel came down the wing and took a slap shot that scored. His was a similar situation to mine. We didn't have as much talent, but we had drive that was unmatched. Every time on the ice, we didn't want to let down our coach or our team."

Snow may have been the most motivated player on the ice. He'd played poorly in his team's 8–1 drubbing by Hendricken a few weeks earlier and feared he might get pulled from the starting position. "My mom and dad were there to pick up the pieces," says Snow, who parlayed his senior year at Mount into a solid college and NHL career. "My mom and dad said, 'Don't worry, Coach Belisle will let you back in.' I practiced my ass off and was in the next game."

Snow was accustomed to battling back from setbacks. His career, to that point, had been inauspicious, and after three seasons, he'd spent much of his time battling for a position on the junior varsity squad while avoiding Coach Bill's doghouse.

"Like a rash, I kept coming back," Snow chuckles. "They challenged me… my games were my practices. Tony Ciresi was my goalie coach. Whenever I let in a goal, they would change the net [replace the goalie]. You'd sprint to the box, and there were four or five goalies waiting. There was no such thing as a good goal. There's no better feeling than getting challenged by Bill Belisle and succeeding. It creates a tight bond when success follows."

Snow, today the general manager of the New York Islanders, says he responded well not only to Bill Belisle but also to other hard-nosed coaches such as the late University of Maine head coach Sean Walsh and NHL coaches Bob Hartley, Mark Crawford and Mike Keenan. Belisle was as tough as they come, says Snow. "I was too scared of [Bill Belisle] to hate him," Snow says with a chuckle. "I had too much respect for him to dislike him. He's demanding; it's his way or the highway. I embraced it. It was my dream as a kid to be a hockey player, to wear the Mount jersey. It was just another step I needed to get to my ultimate goal in life. Now I tell kids, 'Never let anyone tell you you can't do anything.' Mount Saint Charles provided a foundation for who I am today."

MSC also provided an extended family for Snow. When Snow's father, Don, died in 2003, Bill Belisle was there to prop up his former goalie. "It's a family feeling," says Snow, his voice cracking with emotion. "I had a support group that was a family and a coach who helped me to succeed. I have strong emotions of that time."

After the disappointing one-goal loss in the opener, the Mount rallied to beat the Hawks 5–3 in Game 2 to force the rubber match. Steve King gave the Hawks a 1–0 lead after the first period, but it was the only lead the Hawks enjoyed. MSC intensified its forechecking, throttled Emma and Co. in the neutral zone and took control of the game in the second period. Goals by Dave Falls, Jeff Robison and Keith E. Carney gave MSC a 3–1 lead after two periods. Both teams traded a pair of goals in the final period, but Snow stopped at least six point-blank shots (twenty-four saves on the night) late to preserve the win.

Game 3 was one for the ages—if you were a Mount fan. Hendricken took the play to the Mount early, but Snow would not be beaten.

"Garth Snow was the difference," MSC assistant coach Ken Fargnoli told the *Woonsocket Call* after the game. "He literally willed those pucks to not go into the net." Snow had plenty of help. Midway through the opening period, Gaudreau stormed in on Snow. But Gaudreau, with arguably the hardest shot in all of Rhode Island hockey, hit the crossbar.

It was a harbinger of the third period.

MSC took the play to the Hawks. Junior first-line forward Scott Hanley polished off a gorgeous three-on-two by banging home the rebound of Ken Maffia's shot. With twenty-five seconds left in the first period, Hanley was alone in the high slot with the puck and only Hawks' goalie Vin Cardillo before him. Hanley ripped a backhander past the Hendricken netminder to make it 2–0 MSC.

During the life span of The Streak, Mount often benefitted from its superior depth, and players not usually known for their scoring aptitude emerged as series stars. In 1987, Dave Duhamel played that role. Less than two minutes into the second period, Duhamel streaked up the left wing into the Hawks' zone and drove a bullet past Cardillo. The goal made it 3–0 Mount, and suddenly the Hawks fans were silent.

Duhamel today remembers "one of the three greatest moments of my life" as if it had happened yesterday: "I crossed the red line and got a feed from Jason Lawton. I hit the face-off circle and…I was just fortunate that it went in. I was ecstatic, just happy to get the goal to win the series."

As the game progressed, however, Duhamel's marker looked anything like a title-winner. Hendricken, shaken to life by Mount's offensive uprising, stormed back on goals from Emma and Gaudreau to make it 3–2 MSC after two. Emma, late in the period, clanged a shot off the left post, and the Mounties survived a Hawks power play to escape to the dressing room, exhausted but up by one.

"There was tremendous pressure to keep the streak going," says Duhamel. "We had the best goalie in New England, if not the country."

In the third period, Snow played as if he were vying for a Vezina Trophy. As the Hawks faithful roared and cried for their team to score the game-tying goal, Snow refused to be beaten. And when a shot did get by him, a goal post or crossbar came to the rescue. Even with Cardillo pulled for an extra skater, Hendricken could not beat Snow.

"Our depth and players and staff helped us to bond," explains Duhamel. "Mount Pride kept us going. We did it for the benefit of the fans. You just go out there and give it your all. It's nerve-racking for you and for the team. You do it more for your teammates and the fans and the coaches."

Chapter 11
# NOTHING LASTS FOREVER: KING TITANS END THE STREAK

The world did not end, even when The Streak did, in 2004.

The Mount seniors and their teammates respectfully shook the hands of the players that represented the new titans of Rhode Island: Toll Gate High School. Life on Logee Street, it seems, was about to return to normal—or as normal as life can be for a Mount hockey player. After all, when you get right down to it, we're talking about kids playing hockey, not icons defining the sports psyche of a community....

The Mount Mystique, for one season, anyway, was not omnipotent, unlike the Toll Gate offense, led by the dominating Cavanagh cousins, defenseman Dave and forward John. The Titans' titans dominated the ice while goalie Brad Valois won the war between the pipes to lead Toll Gate to a stunning sweep (4–3, 4–0) of the Mounties en route to the 2003–04 Rhode Island state championship. It was Toll Gate's first Division I hockey championship. Conversely, it was Mount's first state championship series defeat since 1977.

The Titans took the opener when John Cavanagh scored his third goal of the night with less than two minutes remaining in regulation. In the decisive game, Valois turned aside twenty-three Mount shots, helping him earn both the shutout and the series MVP. Toll Gate's defense, its strong suit, kept Mount operating from the perimeter, and the MSC machine never got its gears in motion.

When the final horn blared on the history-making season, Dave Belisle took a deep breath and experienced a sense of equanimity despite the

# A History of Mount Saint Charles Hockey

Between 1981 and 1988, rivals Mount Saint Charles and Bishop Hendricken met seven times for the state title, with MSC winning all seven series. Here, goalie Derek Soter protects the net from a Hendricken foe in 2006. *Photo courtesy of Bill Belisle.*

Andrew Bessette (#11) prepares for the faceoff in a 2007 battle against the Hawks. *Photo courtesy of Bill Belisle.*

Sophomore forward John Guay waits for the puck to drop during a contest in the 2005–06 season. Guay went on to earn all-state honors twice during his career. *Photo courtesy of Bill Belisle.*

defeat. "It was a relief," he says, "to no longer be under the microscope and have the kids playing under the microscope. I thought, 'It's all right. We did all right.'"

Part V

# ANATOMY OF A RIVALRY

As lifeless as a tossed-aside rag doll, David Emma sat on the snowy Meehan Auditorium ice, against the boards before his team's bench. His gloves, which had protected the hands of the best faceoff man in Met A, lay beside him, superfluous, never to be worn in another Bishop Hendricken hockey game. Tears streamed down the cheeks of the state's best hockey player.

"It's not right, just not right," Emma thought. "There's just no way Mount Saint Charles should have beaten us." Emma's thoughts echoed ruefully in the minds of teammate Rob Gaudreau and head coach Don Armstrong, and probably by every other Hawks player and fan who, at around 11:15 that Monday night, felt their life force sucked out of them. Yes, once again, Mount Saint Charles had found a way to beat Hendricken.

Gaudreau, who would carry the torch for the Hawks the following season, today muses about the stunning championship loss in 1987: "There just wasn't enough time"—not enough time to score the game-tying goal against surely the best goalie this side of Quebec, the goalie capital of the world. The goalie was Garth Snow, and between his twenty-four saves, a flurry of pucks that clanged metal and timely scoring from his teammates, MSC had survived the Hawks' third-period onslaught to take Game 3, 3–2, and the 1987 state title.

So when the postgame announcement of the series MVP clanged throughout the standing Meehan Auditorium crowd, David Emma was in no mood to hear his name called—no mood to be named the first championship series MVP for the losing team since perhaps, well, ever. The Hawks had come up short, and that's all that mattered to Emma.

Like a dad steeling his son against bitter disappointment, head coach Don Armstrong encouraged his star player to do the right thing.

"David, get up and get the trophy," Armstrong told Emma.

"No, coach. I don't want that one; I want the other one," Emma blurted between snorts and sobs.

Armstrong refused to back down. Emma had played like the series' most valuable player, and now he needed to act like it, even in the wake of the crushing defeat.

"David, you gotta get up and get the MVP trophy," Armstrong said firmly.

"I don't want to, Coach."

"You're going to get up and get that trophy—let's go!" ordered Armstrong, with a sense of finality.

Then a strange thing happened. When Emma rose first from the ice and then from his own grief and finally skated over to accept the MVP trophy, Hendricken fans stood en masse and gave him a standing ovation. Then the unlikely followed: the Mount faithful joined the Hawks fans in warmly and respectfully saluting the state's best hockey player. The outpouring of appreciation underscored the respect shared by these two giants of hockey since their initial title series meeting in 1981. "The thing that made the rivalry so great was the mutual respect we had for each other's team and the team's fans had for the other school," says former Hawks head coach Don Armstrong. "The Mount kids were saying, 'You bums, you bums, go back to the slums'…and the Hendricken kids had their chant: 'You hicks, you hicks, go back to the sticks.'"

In the 1980s, when the two teams fought jealously for the state title seven times, Rhode Island hockey became not just a New England power but also a national titan. From the 1979–80 season through 1989, MSC was ranked tops in the country. Many of those years, Hendricken finished in the top ten, even the top five. LaSalle Academy and Cranston East also made appearances in the nation's top twenty. From these exceptional teams emerged all-star clubs and offseason travel teams composed of players who'd made headlines playing against each other in the RIIL. Now, gilt-edged players such as Robison and Gaudreau and many others were wearing the same jerseys. Hockey enemies became social friends. The '80s were the glorious years for Rhode Island hockey teams and players, and from that era emerged a unique rivalry between Hendricken and Mount Saint Charles.

Dave Duhamel, who scored what proved to be the game- and championship-winning goal in the 1987 series versus Hendricken, remembers the unusual relationship between players from these two programs: "We were happy to win, but it was disheartening to see the other team lose. "It's a long season… you almost get spoiled expecting the Mounties to win. Some take it for granted—both fans and younger players. Emma, Gaudreau…they are still friends. We have had a mutual respect."

"It was two schools that attracted some of the best athletes in the state, and there was always a constant battle to be the one holding the [championship] trophy," says Emma. "I have nothing but tremendous memories of the challenge we faced that time—to beat the mighty Mount Saint Charles. Keith Carney and Garth Snow, we played together in youth hockey in battles before. You loved having them as teammates, but you hated playing against them. There was a lot of respect."

Respect, yes, but for many Hendricken players, there was also a sense of regret and lasting emptiness. Rob Gaudreau, especially, has long regretted not winning a state title. A Lincoln native, Gaudreau likely would have won four state titles had he stayed local and chosen Mount over Hendricken. However, Gaudreau says that he considered Hendricken and head coach Don Armstrong better suited to his academic and athletic strengths and goals. "Most of my friends in youth hockey went to Hendricken," says Gaudreau. "I don't regret it at all. My biggest disappointment was never winning a high school state championship, but life moved on. As time goes by, losing in the finals is insignificant compared to the friendships you made and what you learned in college and in games."

After graduating from high school, Gaudreau starred at Providence College, where his teammates included former Mounties Jeff Robison, Brian Jefferies and Brian Ridolfi. To this day, he and Robison attend concerts together and share cocktails. "During and after college, he and I were the concert guys," Gaudreau says with a chuckle. "We usually invited the other if one of us was going."

Doubtless, such familiarity of and friendship between players and the two teams fueled the rivalry. Unlike today, when many players have myriad academic and athletic options, in the 1980s, the typical Rhode Islander grew up dreaming of wearing Mount red, blue and white; Hendricken green and gold; or LaSalle maroon. To don the sweater of your favorite team was, like former Mountie Charlie Mandeville explained, tantamount to wearing the cape of a superhero. Come playoff time, that sense of power grew tenfold, it seemed. That's how Mount was able to recover from an 8–1 loss to Hendricken in the 1986–87 regular season to win the state title.

"[With] playoff hockey…the level of intensity and the will to fight go up exponentially," says Emma. "I think that was the difference. When everything is on the line, the great players and teams compete at such a high level; that's what makes it so fun."

While his players waged war with their Mountie counterparts, Hendricken coach Don Armstrong waged his own battle with master strategist Bill Belisle.

"MSC really pushed me and my players to be better," says Armstrong. "It was tough to coach against Bill Belisle because he had his players in fantastic shape—better shape than the condition I had mine in because of the whole system at Mount Saint Charles, with the rink and their ice time. They would practice for hours. They had their power play down pat."

Doubtless, the additional reps afforded the Mount staff to adjust to their opponents, to repair flaws in their system and to completely assimilate a scheme. But equally key in Mount's mastery of the Hawks in the 1980s was Mount's psychological superiority over Hendricken. Both Gaudreau and Armstrong recall how difficult it was to put the Mounties away. Gaudreau recalls, "At times in the finals, everything went Mount's way. Even after we were done, and I went to PC and then back to Brown for the finals, it was such a confidence. If it was close, Mount was going to win. I didn't think that way until after it [the finals] was over."

"There's pressure," says Armstrong. "There's a feeling toward the end of the game on our part that we're running out of time. We always knew that to keep Mount close to you, you had to make it to the second period. Most of their games, the turning point was about halfway through the second period, when the other team starts to get a little fatigued; that's when Mount really rules. The start of the second period, it's 2–1, and at the end, it's 5–1. I always told the players, 'Make it through the end of that second period and get them even or get them down by just one going into the third, because it's still a game, and maybe they'll be the one to tighten up.' We had nothing to lose."

Most years, Mount had the better players, the better conditioning and, especially in 1987 and 1988, the better bounces. That was also the case in another heartbreaking series before a packed house at Meehan Auditorium and a highly charged atmosphere. By 1983, anti-Mount fans had grown weary of The Streak. It was time for a change. It was time for, as Armstrong puts it, "the funeral of the Mount hockey team."

The series went the distance, down to the final period, and was highlighted by a sequence that could have swung the series in favor of the Hawks. With the scored tied, Hawks all-state senior Peter McGeough blazed into the Mount zone on a breakaway. Mount all-star goalie Alan Perry eased out of the crease, defying McGeough to beat him. A future twelfth-round draft pick of the New York Islanders in the 1983 NHL draft, McGeough unleashed a wicked slap shot that zipped past Perry. What followed deserves a page in Aesop's fables. The puck hit the top of the crossbar with such force that the rubber disk split in two. The individual pieces soared into the air and then in two divergent directions into the stands. The Hawks came no closer to beating MSC, which held on to win its sixth consecutive title.

It's not difficult to imagine Mount hockey alumni benefiting throughout their lives from the competitive challenge posed by Hendricken. The value of the Mount-Hendricken rivalry has also paid dividends for Hendricken alumni who engaged in—and lost—the battles of the 1980s.

At just five-foot-eight, David Emma grew up battling criticism that he was too small to play hockey. The MVP of the 1987 RIIL series, Emma went on to star at Boston College and won the 1990–91 Hobey Baker Award, as collegiate hockey's best player. He played for the 1992 U.S. Olympic team and then enjoyed a ten-year professional hockey career. Today, he is a managing director and partner with HighTower in Naples, Florida, and employs lessons learned from playing against MSC. "It's all those experiences," says Emma. "They groomed me…made me the person and father I am today. Both of our kids are really good athletes. Every day, everything is about being better, and it's the same at work. It's not about the dollars; it's about being the best at everything you do. To this day, it's always humbling when someone comes up and asks you to sign cards or letters and tells you how you impacted their child's life. If I can be a role model, I appreciate it. I want to carry it through life that way."

Led by senior all-state defenseman and captain Steve Snizek (back row), the 2001–02 Mount club celebrates another state championship. *Photo courtesy of Bill Belisle.*

Part VI

# THE CULTURE OF MOUNT SAINT CHARLES HOCKEY

When you sit in the stands at Adelard Arena, ogle at the wall of championship banners and then get hypnotized by the blur of red, blue and white that is the Mount hockey team during warm-ups, it's easy to buy into the illusion that Mount Saint Charles Academy *is* its boys hockey team. Those with perspective, however, know better. The academy is, first and foremost, a living vessel of Faith filled for decades by the Brothers of the Sacred Heart; MSC's approach to academics and athletics serves the entire individual and not just the student. Simply put, to win a state hockey championship at MSC, you first must succeed in the academy's chapel, then its classrooms and, finally, in its arena.

"It's the era of Mount Pride, not Mount hockey pride," says attorney John Harwood, former Rhode Island Speaker of the House and ex-MSC hockey star. "Hockey is a part of the school; the school is not part of the hockey program. We have a really excellent education. We put young men and women out to excellent

A hug says it all. Mount co-coach Bill Belisle embraces senior forward Peter Cook moments after Mount captured the 2013 state title. *Photo courtesy of Ernest Brown.*

schools and careers. I always felt the school was always behind all its programs. MSC got me into an Ivy League school (University of Pennsylvania). It's the academics that make the marketability of the person. That gets overlooked with a program like Mount because of the success of hockey. It's important to give the best—that's what I learned at Mount. It's a tough, cruel world out there. Athletics make you tougher."

What follows are stories of former Mount hockey players who have seen through the illusion that Mount Saint Charles Academy is just a hockey factory but who realize that it is first and foremost a vital culture and community preparing its students for life.

## Chapter 12
# JOHN GUEVREMONT, CLASS OF 1976: SPREADING THE WORD(S)

"What Mount hockey did was make me know and love Mount, and I have been there thirty-three years," says John Guevremont, a former MSC defenseman and, today, an English teacher at the academy. Approaching his mid-fifties, Mr. Guevremont is best known by his students for his passion for writing and literature and, not infrequently, diversions with his students into deep and meaningful discussions of their Catholic faith.

"Religion…the role here is huge," he says. "Besides the fact that we have religion classes, our students do service every single year. It's just amazing how many opportunities they have to do service for the elderly and handicapped kids. I'm a pretty spiritual person, and I don't ever hesitate to talk about my faith in class. Some kids say this is as much a religion class as it is an English class. A lot of teachers like that kids don't see religion separate from school, from life. It's not an awkward thing at all. Most of the teachers that get hired do it because they love to celebrate their religious beliefs."

Teaching at the Mount not only fortified Guevremont's spiritual foundation; it also opened his eyes to other previously occluded artistic attributes. First, he discovered that he had the pipes for singing, the sensibilities to teach himself how to play piano and the creative muse to write music. Combine these artistic elements, and you have an English teacher who's been the lead singer of a rock band for seven years and a writer who, despite being unable to read music, has written two complete musicals that have been performed at Mount. Not bad for a kid who, like many hockey players, struggled mightily to perform up to Bill Belisle's expectations.

# A History of Mount Saint Charles Hockey

"When I think back, my father [Marcel] said, 'Why did you play hockey? You have this gift for music, and you spent hours and hours and hours playing hockey. My father always wanted to be a hockey player, so he got his kids into it. For me, it took up all of my time, but there are important lessons you learn when you play sports—teamwork, accomplishment. But I can't say that Mount hockey made me into the person I am today at all."

Perhaps not. But the allure of the larger-than-life Mount players and teams opened the door through which Guevremont envisioned a future in the arts and literature.

Odds are that if you were a kid of French Canadian descent, like Guevremont, growing up in Woonsocket in the late 1960s and early 1970s, there was only one game, one sport of note: street hockey. True Woonsocket pucksters went nowhere without their Mylec street hockey stick—a plastic blade heated and curved like a Stan Mikita banana blade. After school, kids transformed their streets into narrow asphalt hockey arenas as they stickhandled rubber balls or worn-out tennis balls past driveways, around cars and between the legs of cats and dogs. They fashioned goals out of two-by-fours and wire, or maybe a little brother's old blanket. Then they toiled until interrupted by a car needing to pull into a driveway or until little brother pedaled up the street on an orange spider bike with the amazingly high motorcycle-style handle bars and screamed, "Mom says it's time to eat!"

Weekends boasted street hockey tournaments that began at sunrise and lasted until it was time to go to school on Monday morning. Weekend tripleheaders were a big deal because the turnout was enormous (you could even play two and three lines). There were even backup goalies, and sometimes girls joined in—a rarity for 1970. Come winter, street hockey games were preempted not because of darkness but because you and the kids needed a lift to 800 Logee Street to watch the only hockey team in the universe, Mount Saint Charles. One boy, around Guevremont's age, even hitchhiked to the arena through wind and snow and all other elements. He risked life and limb and three weeks of punishment because he'd been hypnotized by "The Blur" and by the Saints who marched into Adelard Arena.

Today, Guevremont fondly recalls the transfixing image of the Mount players speeding around the ice during warm-ups in their red-white-and-blue uniforms. "I can remember watching them when they took the ice and flying around the ice. There would be like a strong wind at the speed of them going around the ice, and it was just amazing…especially the warm-ups. These guys were unbelievable. Yes, it was a dream to watch them… the Canadiens' uniforms, the 'When the Saints Go Marching In' from the

# THE CULTURE OF MOUNT SAINT CHARLES HOCKEY

No, your eyes aren't blurry; when a Mount team skates full tilt during pregame warm-ups, it's a sight to behold. *Photo courtesy of Bill Belisle.*

Defenseman Mike Cornell (#19) leads the Mount "Blur." *Photo courtesy of Bill Belisle.*

pep band...Every game I went to, maybe my father took me only to playoff games, but it was always packed. The crowd was just amazingly loud, and I felt—I don't know why—but I felt like they were *my* team. Somehow I had some connection with the school. It was like my first professional team."

Amazed, Guevremont was. Though he was a pretty good youth hockey player, even making the vaunted Rhode Island Kings, Guevremont held little hope for ever playing for MSC. He'd started playing ice hockey when he was ten and still had some catching up to do.

When Mount Saint Charles Junior High opened, Guevremont and many of his teammates from the Woonsocket youth hockey system enrolled. They would soon form the heart of the 1975–76 teams, the Woonsocket Connection.

Guevremont was, by his own admission, "tentative" and afraid to make a miscue at the blue line. Still, he cracked the starting lineup as a junior and played for Steve Shea. The following season, Bill Belisle came on board.

Yikes!

John Guevremont knew "Mr. Belisle." Bill was a distant cousin of the Guevremonts; he'd played hockey with Marcel Guevremont and had coached John in youth hockey, along with his own sons. John knew how demanding Coach Bill could be—could he instill in John Guevremont the confidence and decision-making skills the defenseman needed to succeed at Mount?

"It was that competitive in my senior year," says Guevremont. "It was pretty much where every practice, every game, you are under scrutiny. Every game, your best is always demanded. I guess that's when you aren't a superstar, and you aren't going to be a great goal scorer, so you never really win your position. You're on red defense and then after the game you are suddenly told to wear a white jersey in practice—you've have been demoted."

Many players skating on the thin ice between failure and success experience an epiphany or a key moment that swings the pendulum to favor success. Guevremont's career-changing moment occurred during a scrimmage early in his senior year. For this practice game, Belisle had deferred coaching duties to an assistant. Without Belisle's ubiquitous presence, Guevremont played with fearless abandon, showcasing dazzling stickhandling skills. The tentative kid could really play! Ironically, as Guevremont jingled and jangled with the puck, Coach Bill watched from an obscured vantage point in the arena. Guevremont recalls:

# The Culture of Mount Saint Charles Hockey

*I played a little more relaxed...I could carry the puck quite well, except for fear that with Mr. Belisle, if you ever carried the puck and lost it and a goal was scored, you were in big trouble. The next practice, he called me over to his office and said, 'Why don't you play like that for me?" "What do you mean?" I said. "You played fearlessly and were very, very shifty, and you can carry the puck. I want you to carry the puck." I was shocked. I did, and the first thing you know, I was on the power play, and shorthanded, and he told me to put on a white jersey, and I was on the first line. That was the epitome of my hockey days: first-line defense.*

For John Guevremont, organized hockey ended when he departed the Mount varsity locker room for the final time. "By the time I left Mount, I felt I had done a lifetime of hockey, and I was ready to retire," says Guevremont. "Was it fun? Umm, is it ever fun? There was always pressure. There was a time when we were pretty good, and we started to get some success and beat a lot of good teams, and I felt very secure for my position. Then it was fun...street hockey was fun! Other things were fun, too. Sometimes there'd be a snow day, and there'd be free ice at Mount and Bill Belisle would call my father and say, "Hey, take the boys," and it would be me and my brother [David], John Belisle, David Belisle and Mr. Belisle on the ice for like two hours for shooting, and that was a lot of fun."

If hockey didn't sate his deepest hunger, teaching English at Mount has. "When I came back to Mount, the hockey players walked on water, and in a way...it gave the school this sense of identity that we have a national profile," says Guevremont. "Shortly after starting to teach, I had Brian Lawton in class, and that was really cool for me...that I had the superstar hockey players and I had instant credibility with the kids because I had been a hockey player."

As the years passed, Guevremont became Chair of the English Department, and his interest in students was based more on their test grades than their goals-against-average.

"It's almost exciting to take a kid who's a hockey player—Brian Lawton, for example, or Paul Pratt. I've had some hockey players that were fabulous students. Hockey's going to be nice, but he's not going to need it because he's going to be able to do anything. I never had a sense of...favoring hockey players. Unfortunately, there was a rumor during the glory years that hockey players were treated especially well by teachers—given breaks and passed when they failed and stuff like that. If anything, many teachers were careful *not* to favor them."

Guevremont admits that during the heyday of The Streak, not all members of the Mount academic family appreciated the public perception that MSC was "the hockey school."

"We're doing so well academically, plus we have other teams that are really good. Since the early 2000s, we built a new gym and converted the old gym to arts and a band room. We have a new dance studio. We actually almost became known as a fine arts school. We would have a lot more kids in the fine arts than we would playing hockey."

Guevremont isn't just investing in the school's academics and fine arts; he's also keeping alive the charism of the Order of the Brothers of the Sacred Heart of New England Inc., whose original educational mission remains the "evangelization of young people."

Guevremont is participating in the Coindre Leadership Program (CLP), a three-year intensive "personal for-mation program" geared to help participants better understand the mission and charism of the Brothers of the Sacred Heart and to train them to mentor others in the charism. In a way, he is becoming a disciple for the Brothers.

"When I was at Mount, I had been bred from Brothers that were really instrumental in shaping me as a student," says Guevremont. "In some ways, I do the same for my students. The Brothers know that there's going to be a day within the next thirty years when there's absolutely no Brothers in New England or at Mount. We're not getting new ones in the United States; they are doing very well in Africa, but not America, not New England. They take laymen, and they train us in the history and the charism of the Brothers so that the spirit of the Brothers lives on."

Chapter 13

# RICHARD LAWRENCE, MSC DIRECTOR OF ATHLETICS: KEEPING SPORTS IN PERSPECTIVE

They're all his kids, really—these teenage boys and girls who shoot pucks and hurl javelins and slam baseballs, whose two-handed backhand shots make it 40–Love, whose layups win in the closing seconds. When these kids on these and other teams comprising Mount Saint Charles athletics prove to be exceptional in their respective sports, they are honored with championship trophies. As the patriarch of MSC school sports, Richard Lawrence's fingerprints remain forever a part of the championship cup.

"For good or for bad, I say to people that these are all my teams, and I have ownership of all of them," says MSC's award-winning athletic director. "I say to my coaches, "The responsibility is immediately with you, but ultimately it's with me." How we succeed and how we fail is a reflection of me doing my job. I have to put the right people in the right places, and I have to get them to understand the philosophies we promote."

Few understand the mission of the school and the athletics as intimately as Lawrence. Since arriving at the Mount campus in 1969, he has served as athletic director, English teacher and soccer and tennis coach. Lawrence holds a CMAA (Certified Master Athletic Administrator) in athletic administration, and he has been inducted into the Rhode Island Boys Soccer Coaches Association Hall of Fame, the Rhode Island Girls Tennis Coaches Association Hall of Fame, the New England Soccer Hall of Fame and the Rhode Island College Athletic Hall of Fame.

In many ways, no award is more in synch with Mount's ethical values than the Rhode Island Interscholastic League's Challenge Cup. Last year, MSC won its fifth consecutive Challenge Cup award, in the Small Division. The award recognizes a school for excellence in all sports, sportsmanship and school spirit. Schools are ranked by a point system based on performance and votes throughout the year.

"I have personal philosophies that I think coincide with the mission of the school…we value the child, we promote good citizenship through sports and, with sports as a vehicle, we promote excellence first and foremost," says Lawrence. "We are trying to mold the entire person. Getting coaches to buy into that is not always easy, for they often have their own vision of what they want to do."

Case in point: Bill Belisle and the Mount boys hockey program. Both Bill Belisle and Richard Lawrence are deeply motivated men with strong convictions, a deeply rooted spiritual faith and a unique ability to express themselves bluntly. Could these two equally proud captains of their individual ships steer together down the same ocean?

"I was here when Bill Belisle began," recalls Lawrence. "There's been an evolution together. He and I have come to understand this evolution in terms of what we prioritize—we believe in the entire evolution of the student. I have seen a much better understanding of this over the years, and as I have evolved in this leadership role, I have seen an understanding on the Belisles' part. They understand what I am saying when I am saying it and why I am doing what I'm doing. To be honest, that wasn't always true in the early going. They are very passionate people, and I am, too. We disagree on some things, but I feel there's a mutual respect, and with that mutual respect there's an understanding of what we're trying to accomplish. An important piece of that is achieving a high level of excellence."

That's why the incident at the end of the 2009–10 championship playoff series against LaSalle Academy was so unusual.

In the waning seconds of what would become a Mount series-clinching 5–2 victory, a fight broke out near the Mount net. When officials had restored order, a Mount player and coach had been ejected from the game. The league later placed the program on probation for the 2010–11 season for unsportsmanlike conduct. In the wake of the incident, Lawrence and the MSC administration and coaching staff met numerous times to ensure no repeat of such behavior. "We teach it [sportsmanship]. You can't assume it; you have to teach it…as well as fan behavior and loyalty. Those are the three components," says Lawrence.

One of the many challenges the Mount athletic director encounters is validating and promoting the school's excellence in other sports, such as

## The Culture of Mount Saint Charles Hockey

tennis, soccer, volleyball and so forth. He admits that it isn't easy but says that no one should begrudge the pucksters—both girls and boys teams—for their success. It all adds to the Mount athletic culture:

> *I hear it all the time: "Oh, yeah, hockey..." But we are successful in many other areas. We are a balanced school with balanced programs. I have been coaching tennis for fifty-three seasons, and both boys and girls have had remarkable success. It's not a marquee sport, and I understand that. Mothers, fathers, sisters, brothers, boyfriends, girlfriends...they come, and that's it. That's what people are interested in, and they deserve all the accolades they get. I take pleasure in every single award, in every single accolade. When Bill Belisle or Dave Belisle or the team is cited for something, I claim a piece of that; I stand up, and I make my chest big. I am very proud of what they bring to the school. We're nationally acclaimed. People know about us around the country, and I am very proud of that. Frozen Fenway* [the 2011 hockey game versus Springfield Cathedral, held at Fenway Park] *was fantastic...such a highlight of the school year. Does it happen to other programs in the school? No—the mechanics aren't there. But for hockey, they are, and we'll take it and say this only makes our school more prominent, more notable and more successful overall.*

Despite the academic and athletic success of the school, students still leave for other opportunities. While the Belisles have adjusted to their annual rotating hockey roster, Lawrence remains puzzled by parents' decisions to send their children off to a boarding prep school:

> *I was talking to a man...his son came here and was an excellent hockey player, and his nephew was also here. Last year, he had his son here and took him out. I said to him, "You have your child for such a short time as a child—you're going to tell me you're going to send him to a prep school? You'll still see him, but it's not the same; he's not under your tutelage, not under your guidance." The gentleman said, "But all this great opportunity he has—the possibility of a scholarship to this school and that school and a better college..." I said, "Is it worth it? You're giving up your kid's childhood?" But he was adamant that it was the right thing to do. Right now, the youngest of my six children is twelve, and I know at eighteen, I'm going to lose him. For me to lose him at fourteen? No way. He's too precious, and my time with him is too precious. I also want him under my guidance. I don't think that's selfish, but that's not how people think, and I*

# A History of Mount Saint Charles Hockey

Head coach Bill Belisle celebrates another Mount record. Belisle holds the national record for most career wins (904), while his clubs set the national standard for consecutive league wins (94) and consecutive state titles (26). Overall, Mount's 43 wins are the most ever by a high school hockey program. *Photo courtesy of Bill Belisle.*

*can't convince people otherwise. There's so many people going off to junior hockey, going off to prep school...when I look at what ultimately happens to them, I don't see any great difference between what they have when they get out of prep school and what they would have had here.*

The majority stay, embrace the Mount culture, graduate and return. Some, like Steve Shea and John Guevremont, return to MSC so that they can share with others their life experiences, their passion for Mount and the spirit of the Brothers that resides in them. Other alumni return to Mount simply to say hello (again) or to honor one of their former mentors.

"I think that when you have an eightieth birthday party for Bill Belisle, and people come back from years ago, that's a physical statement that says there's something that happened when they were there," says Lawrence. "They want to come back after ten, twenty and, for some of them, thirty years to say, 'Happy Birthday!' Something happened. Were their lives changed? I think so."

## Chapter 14
# ED LEE: FROM STREET PUNK TO STUDENT HEALER

The moments that define an individual and plot his future can be as subtle as a whisper or as blunt as a slap in the face. Ed Lee experienced the latter, and it rescued him from potential disaster.

By the third year of his coaching career at Mount, Bill Belisle rarely left his concrete home of Adelard Arena to venture up the hill to the academy. The rink was his; the school belonged to the Brothers of the Sacred Heart. So when Coach Bill strode into the boys locker room at 7:30 a.m. on the first day of the 1977–78 school year, Ed Lee felt the blood drain from his body.

A member of the Mount JV team as a freshman, Lee had done little to show Coach Bill that he was anything more than one of the biggest punks on campus. Now, a year later, Lee wondered what the man most feared around these parts would say—if he said anything.

Sure enough, as Lee stood outside his locker, the czar of MSC hockey got in his face. He glared into the cowering boy's wide eyes—perhaps even into his soul. Belisle growled succinctly, and the words became Lee's lifesaving slap in the face: "You'll never make my team. You're not a good enough skater. You'll never handle the academics here. I want you to transfer."

Transfer where? Lee's mind began to spin with the ramifications of Belisle's words. With tears welling in his eyes, Lee sniffled, "Coach, I got nowhere else to go."

Coach Belisle did have someplace else to go, however. He spun on his heels and marched out the door and out of sight—for the moment. His pronouncement was a painful alarm in Lee's ears, mind and, fortunately, his heart.

Ed Lee refused to leave MSC, refused to give up, refused to go back to the streets of Providence, with its gangs and its drugs and its vagrancy and its daily serving of futility. With Coach Bill's challenge a part of his emotional fiber, Ed Lee soon took his first steps from displaced street punk to healer and mentor of children a generation later. In between the tongue lashing from Coach Bill and his current career in education, Lee became a Mount all-star, the first Belisle-coached player drafted by an NHL club, a star forward at Princeton and a member of the U.S. National Team. How Lee bridged these two disparate lives is a story in itself, and it begins, oddly enough, with a jacket. "When I was in second grade, I had someone take my jacket off me when I was on the bus, and I never forget it," he says.

But Lee almost lost more than just his jacket that day—he nearly lost his childhood.

By her twenty-first birthday, Lena Lee had had five children, including Ed. She moved her son and four daughters thirteen times in sixteen years because the family simply could not afford the rents. In fact, Ed Lee spent the last four years of his childhood sleeping on the porch/bedroom of his grandmother's house that had electricity but no heat. In many ways, Lena Lee was both mother and father to her children. Her husband, Ed Lee Sr., a landscaper by trade, had been a gifted athlete in his youth and had played hockey for LaSalle before transferring to Hope High School. A talented boxer while serving in the army, Lee Sr. also was a whiz at chess. Despite his many natural gifts, he also was an alcoholic who often neglected his family.

Without the proper familial support and direction, Ed Lee strayed into the seedy and shadowy streets of Providence. He looked one way and saw the East Side Gang; there were the ruffians from Camp Street; Lord knows you didn't step one foot in the North End with the Italians or over to Fox Points. Bullies here, bullies there, bullies everywhere, all with their own jealously guarded turf. But around the corner was the great equalizer, the great hockey building: the Rhode Island Auditorium.

"The crew I did hang around with...most of them were into sports, so sports was the great equalizer," says Lee. We were in trouble, but we also played sports every single day. My grandfather owned the old Penalty Box [bar] next to the auditorium. It was called Lee's Café. I come from a family of alcoholics, which is why I haven't had a drink since I was about twenty-five. I came out of a bar one night and got busted up and said that's enough for me. I don't want to be like my father. My father drank for a good twenty-five years. I brought him to two rehabs; he used to come home all busted up all time."

Sure, Lee and his streetwise friends played hockey, but they also stole practically anything that wasn't nailed to the floor. One day, he and another pal sneaked into a home owned by a doctor. From there, they lifted a few guitar cases and a violin. Of course, what was a kid no more than thirteen or fourteen years old going to do with a hot fiddle? Sell it. Unfortunately, that was a pricey Stradivarius violin, worth thousands of dollars. The hot violin circulated from owner to owner until an undercover cop traced the deal back to Lee and placed him under arrest.

By age fifteen, Lee had been cuffed four times and was looking at a future in a penalty box lined with bars. That's when the far-reaching shadow of Bill Belisle began to edge its way into Lee's life. After his fourth arrest and expulsion from his third school, Lee appeared before a juvenile court judge who would decide Lee's future. Rather than sentence him to a detention facility, the judge gave Lee one final chance at redemption by ordering him to enroll at Mount Saint Charles. After all, for years the academy and its hard-nosed Brothers had straightened out kids like Lee who needed a firm hand and a caring nature. Surely Bill Belisle could provide the structure and direction Lee needed.

In his freshman year, Lee got a taste of the shocking diet of reality that Belisle dished out in platefuls.

"My freshman year, I had a friend up there who flunked out," remembers Lee. "I played fourth-line JV. My sophomore year comes around, and everybody's scared to death of Bill Belisle. The reputation he had was that of a drill sergeant. The thing about Bill Belisle was that he wasn't in it for any selfish reasons—he wasn't in it to get his name in the paper or in the limelight. He wasn't in it to make any money; he was in it because he loved ice hockey. He knew ice hockey because he came from Quebec, where hockey was a religion. He was built on speed, hustle and proper positioning. That's what he did: drill. Drill repetitions every day."

Some thirty-seven years later, even Lee is uncertain why Belisle asked him to leave the team. Sure, Lee did not skate well, and his buddy had flunked out of school a year earlier. Had Belisle merely concluded that flunkies came in pairs? Or was the crafty Belisle challenging Lee to dig down inside himself and live up to his potential?

Whatever Bill Belisle's motivation, it worked. Lee began to apply himself, both in the classroom and on the ice. Coach became a mentor, pushing Lee, encouraging him to bulk up and improve his skating. To fail in the classroom was to return to the streets of Providence a failure. So desperate to succeed was Lee that for the first eighteen months at Mount, he hitchhiked to and from school every day, thumbing his way up and down the oft-deserted Route 146, because no one was available or able to provide him with transportation. Eventually, Lee Sr. used one year's tax refund to purchase a car for his son.

With Belisle's support and his own perseverance, Lee climbed the ladder and made the Mount varsity his sophomore season, 1978. That year, he played with line mates Bob Cardignan and future Olympian Paul Guay as the Mount beat LaSalle in three games to win its first state title since 1972. The high-powered Mounties also grabbed the New England Championship, which was held only a few miles from Lee's home in Providence.

What followed after the game is one of the many anecdotes that illustrate Coach Belisle's eternal maxim: the team comes before the individual. Lee remembers:

> *He would never break a rule on anything. You had your rules, and you abided by them. Case in point: my sophomore year, we're playing at Brown University in the New England Championship. I lived a block from Brown. We win the championship at Brown, and the season is over. I asked Larry [assistant coach Larry Tremblay], "Can I go home with my mother?" He asks Belisle, who says "Nope, you take the bus back to Woonsocket. You get someone to pick you up in Woonsocket, and they take you back." "But I live a block from here—my mother doesn't have a car!" I don't even know if he knew how he was affecting everybody. Those first few years he was there, I don't think he thought about that. I think he had so much tunnel vision with his military training…he just loved hockey so much.*

Then again, when Coach Bill complimented you, the feeling of relief and joy seemed to last for an entire season.

"My sophomore year, he came up to me on the bus when we had lost our first game and said, 'I like your stick work out there,'" recalls Lee. "It was the first thing he said to me all year. I was on third line; I was doing alright."

The following year, Lee emerged as one of the team's best forwards. He was a second team all-state selection, and he led MSC to its first undefeated season and second straight title. These were the first of the heady days of Mount hockey. But Lee and his teammates knew better than to wax cocky. "After my junior year, when we beat LaSalle the second time, a couple of a LaSalle players came into our locker room and said, 'You're starting a dynasty here.' In the back of our minds, we'd say, 'Yeah.' But we never said that aloud because Belisle preached humility: you never say anything to the referees, you don't question the coaches, you don't say anything at all. You keep your mouth shut. When you jump over those boards, you go full speed or you're not on my time."

Ed Lee had jumped over not just the boards at Brother Adelard Arena but also the barriers from a few years before. Belisle and the Brothers of the Sacred Heart had taken Lee off the street and had eradicated its ugly temptations from Lee's mind and soul. He entered his senior year ready for the breakout campaign expected of him. However, prior to the hockey season, the Rhode Island Interscholastic League passed a rule that prohibited athletes from participating in sports for no more than four consecutive seasons. Lee had repeated his freshman year, thus making him ineligible to play any sports his senior year at Mount.

For a Mount hockey player, the senior year is one to make a personal statement, to be a leader of the undergraduates, to ensure that Mount Pride lives on. Ed Lee could only watch his former teammates win their third straight title in 1980. Still, as he learned in years to come, the Brothers and Bill Belisle had started him on a successful college and professional career.

Lee parlayed his hockey experience and education at Mount into a sociology degree from Princeton University, even recording straight A's his senior year. During those four years, Lee also began to utilize some of Coach Belisle's training techniques designed to improve his skating stride and speed. They worked.

Lee became the first Mountie drafted by an NHL club (Quebec, fifth round, 1981 draft). Moreover, he was selected to the U.S. National and the 1984 Olympic traveling teams. After the 1980 "Miracle on Ice" at Lake Placid, expectations were high for the 1984 Olympic squad. Lee, a member of the twenty-seven-man Olympic team in the summer of 1983, however, believed he would not make the final cut and therefore returned to Princeton for his senior year.

Lee played professional hockey, briefly, in the International and American Hockey leagues, along with two European leagues.

Regardless of his location, Lee maintained Belisle's grueling physical training regimen. "He trains you so hard that your body gets used to it," he says. "Wherever I was, I was always writing letters thanking him."

Today, exactly five and a half miles separate Ed Lee from yesterday and today, from being a victim to being a healer. "I've come a three-quarter circle," says Lee, now in his early fifties. "I'm right where I should be now." Geographically, "where I should be" is 674 Prairie Avenue in Providence, site of the Sgt. Cornel Young Jr. & Charlotte Woods Elementary School at the B. Jae Clanton Complex, where Lee is assistant principal. The two-story redbrick building is a mere handful of side streets and a brief ride up I-95 from Lee's thirteenth and final childhood home on Fourth Street. Most people his age who'd suffered through countless trials and tribulations of youth would feel inclined to run away from a forgettable childhood. Lee chooses to virtually complete a cycle of life by returning to the streets where gangs once ruled and fought so that he can save kids before they, like him, end up standing before a judge in juvenile court. After completing his hockey career, Lee accepted a position as a juvenile counselor at the Rhode Island Training school, a job that was short-lived and grueling, working with kids "on their way to the ACI [Rhode Island Adult Correctional Institute], most of them." Uncertain of his next move, he returned to college and added a history degree and teaching certification. He then returned to Providence, and the classroom, ready to help at-risk kids. His mantra for them: "You can get over it; you can make it."

Lee's first chance to apply that mantra came with his first significant teaching appointment—that of a disabled sixteen-year-old African American girl:

> *I was working at Central High School as a substitute teacher, and the department head asked me if I wanted to do some at-home instruction. I said, "Sure." I come to find out the home instruction was at a hospital. Apparently, this sixteen-year-old girl was outside at a birthday party when a kid came up and asked her to dance. She said no, and he went out to his car, came back and shot her in the neck—and then he shot another kid, too. He was never found, but she was left a quadriplegic.*
>
> *There I was at the hospital with her, watching her sipping out of a straw. I became friends with the mother, who had to take a bus there every day. I ended up getting close with her. I did a fundraiser for the girl and raised a bunch of money...got her a computer and a handicapped van and actually got her back to school in her wheelchair. She came to school for a year and a half and graduated. I knew her ten more years...she died about a year ago. Ten years...and her mother said all she used to do was sing these angelic songs at night...my first real situation.*

And there was yet another life lesson for Ed Lee, for she taught him about spirit, love and gratitude—three linchpins of life he holds precious to this day. "You realize how lucky you are," he says. "All she ever did was say no to a dance at a birthday party."

They aren't all like that special girl. Over the years, Lee has taught kids who wanted for nothing and others who were practically bereft of education and financial and familial stability. "But I wonder who needs the help the most. The kids who have everything handed to them—can they stand on their own feet later on? Everyone needs help. That's why I am in a real good situation where I am now."

Today, Lee ensures his students have the same chance for success that the Mount gave him. What does he try to impart to his kids? That every individual has his or her own personality, his or her own strengths and his or her own weaknesses. "They all have gifts," he says. "You have to find the gifts, but you've got to have backups. I explain to them that it's all about how hard you work. If you want something, you can get it."

Working with students in grades K–5 affords Lee the opportunity to right their wrongs before they get caught in life's downward spiral. From the get-go, he made it clear to the students at Young and Woods that there would be one path to righteousness and that it was based on mutual respect. No one would, metaphorically, steal a classmate's jacket.

"When I first started here, there were six or seven bullies I brought down to my office," recalls Lee. "I marched them down there, hands behind their back. I got on the phone and called my friend who I used to work with as a

Mount co-coach Dave Belisle addresses members of the 2006 squad. *Photo courtesy of Bill Belisle.*

police officer, and I got him on the speakerphone. Within thirty seconds, all the kids were crying. I explained to them that bullying is against the law. I kept a good eye on those kids, and they changed."

They had an apt role model in Ed Lee, whose transformation from street punk to life coach has benefitted dozens of others in his life. The year Lee was accepted to Princeton, his father quit drinking. Father and son enjoyed a healthy, happy sober relationship until Ed Lee Sr.'s death nine years ago. Meanwhile, to honor his mother's courage and perseverance, seven years ago, Lee started the Rena Lee Perseverance Award, which raises money to help kids overcome obstacles in life.

"I'm in a good situation," says Lee. "I got out of a bad environment, got great teachers and great coaches and got lucky. And Bill Belisle saved my life."

Chapter 15

# IT'S A FAMILY AFFAIR: THE INFLUENCE OF MOUNT HOCKEY ON JOHN, BILL, DAVE AND PETER BELISLE

The 1989–90 hockey season opened with MSC facing more internal challenges than any Mount team had since the outset of The Streak. It had just captured its twelfth straight title and its tenth (and final) consecutive national championship. Mount also had graduated the five best players in the state: forwards Brian Jefferies, Brian Ridofi, and Derek Chauvette and defensemen Brendan Whittet and Keith P. Carney—the "Big Five," as they were known on Logee Street. Replacing them would be a challenge for Bill Belisle; his new club returned a number of solid players but none with the natural talent of the Big Five. For the Mount to keep The Streak alive, core players such as Peter Belisle were expected to take their next step up the ladder. For the first time, the spotlight shined brightly on senior Peter Belisle, son of Coach Bill and little brother of Dave and John Belisle.

"The Streak...there's so much pressure," recalls Peter. "I'm the coach's son; I can't lose it. I gotta do something about that."

Peter Belisle was accustomed to stickhandling through Belisle-imposed pressure. He'd grown up watching his father win state title after state title and had seen his brother Dave turn promising JV players into varsity stars.

"All I wanted was to put on the Mount jersey. I started out as the water boy, the stick boy, the manager. I was around Mount constantly."

As a pre-teen, when Adelard Arena ice was available to those with the right connections, Peter Belisle took advantage of the opportunity to practice his heroes, such as future NHL star Mat Schneider, who drilled Peter until his

From Mite star to high school all-state star—a snapshot of 2013 Mount captain Brian Belisle during his youth hockey days with the Woonsocket North Stars. *Photo courtesy of Bill Belisle.*

feet ached. "I would make believe that I had won the Stanley Cup or that I had scored a goal at Mount," remembers Belisle fondly.

Though he had the Belisle DNA and the passion for Mount, as a freshman, Peter lacked the skill to make it on the varsity team. When tryouts came around, Bill Belisle pulled no punches when it came to his son: "My father said to me, 'I know what you can do—you can try out for the jayvees.' I looked up to Dave my whole life. Often, he was like an uncle to me. I looked for my father's approval. It was a little scary because there was a lot of pressure. I wanted it bad, and I think my father and Dave knew this. They had to be tougher on me. The hockey community is small, and I think they were tougher on me because they knew I could take it. My father would clock you over the head with a stick—'Wake up, you dummy!' You couldn't do that in this era."

Peter needed two seasons of JV seasoning before he had the skills to skate a regular shift on the Mount varsity, usually on the third line. He showed promise during his junior season; he was a smart player with good ice vision, and he knew what to do with the puck, where he should be playing on the ice and how to back-check with trademark MSC relentlessness. But his slow feet and soft frame prevented him from playing on one of the team's top two lines. As a senior, however, Belisle and his teammates both expected him and needed him to be a leader. He started the season as the first-line center, fending off pal Dave Curtis, who'd made a name for himself by scoring four goals in Mount's 9–2 title-clinching win over LaSalle the previous year. Suffice it to say, Belisle believed he had completed a lifelong dream by

# The Culture of Mount Saint Charles Hockey

Members of the MSC 2003 senior class are pictured during the 2002–03 season. They went on to lead the Mounties to their final championship during the program's illustrious twenty-six-year state title winning skein. *Photo courtesy of Bill Belisle.*

earning the top pivot spot. But being a first-line center requires more than pedigree, heart and hard work; it takes quick feet, both up and down the ice, as well the brawn to battle for position in the slot. Peter Belisle possessed some of those attributes, but not enough.

Early in the season, Bill Belisle monitored his youngest son in his role and considered the talent distribution among his four forward lines. He made a decision that, for most fathers, would be heartrending—but not for Coach Bill, who played no favorites. Belisle moved his son Peter to the second line and bumped Curtis up to the first line. Not surprisingly, the move worked. Belisle's savvy and strong passing skills improved the second line, while Curtis's speed, size and scoring touch helped to create a bona fide first line. Belisle and Curtis performed their roles to perfection, but Belisle had to swallow his pride, and it hurt going down. "It was tough between us that year," he admits. "Teams are successful because each player has a role and knows it. Finding a role on the team at Mount Saint Charles is very important. A third-line player knew his job; they made it crystal clear. When you do your job, there's value in that. They cultivated that. Back when I played, the fourth-liners dressed but didn't play; they had twelve-minute periods [then], and the fourth-line role was to cheer. If you're not screaming, yelling, being positive for your teammates, you don't dress. No moping allowed. You cheer even if you aren't getting the glory. It can be very hard."

It's hard when it's your father screaming at you or tapping you on the helmet and calling you a dummy if you made, well, a bonehead play. But unlike his older brother Dave, who struggled initially with his father's approach, Peter understood his father's message and motivation. "We're human beings, and sometimes you take it personally," he says. "They're delivering a message. The assistant coaches are great. They come over there…it's the message, not the delivery. Now Dad and Dave's roles are reversed. Dad will call a kid into the office and say, 'I know he [Dave] went bananas, but you gotta do it better, and here's why…' I did love being out there. The hard work is not fun; it's the reward you get from the success—from winning that big game or scoring that big goal. It's a battle to work hard every day, but then, at the end of the day, you look in the mirror at how proud you are of yourself."

Tony Ciresi was a Mount assistant coach from 1980 to 1990. Like other assistants, he was there to prop up a player with shaky self-confidence and to

Two-time NHL all-star defenseman Mat Schneider donned the Mount colors for an alumni game. *Photo courtesy of Bill Belisle.*

remind him of the message behind Coach Belisle's instruction. "I would pull kids aside and explain what they were screwing up," says Ciresi. "Bill ran the show. I did all of my coaching at JV ice time getting them ready for varsity and evaluating guys to move up. If I recommended a guy to move up, he had to be ready to go, otherwise I'd get my ass chewed out. I also coached the junior high. I was especially tough on them because they had to know what it was like when Bill was around. I did spend a good deal of time propping the guys up psychologically. They could really get down. Lots of guys have told me they would have transferred if I hadn't been there. My job was to call them on Saturday to tell them they were out of the lineup. That was a fun festival."

Peter Belisle not only received and applied his father's messages; today, he uses many of those same elements as a coach. Twenty-three years after leading the Mounties to the 1989–90 title (lucky number thirteen of The Streak), Belisle just completed his seventh year as head coach of the UMass Boston men's hockey program. His players have gotten a taste of the Belisle style, ala Peter Belisle.

"It's a blessing what hockey's done for me," says Belisle, a four-year letter winner as a player for the University of Connecticut. "I believe it all happened for a reason. I am doing what I was called to do: coach college hockey full time."

In the days when John Belisle played hockey for his father and the Mount, you expected tough—even brutal—practices that occasionally scared kids from the program. That was expected. Yet for John Belisle, even the most merciless Mount practice was child's play in contrast to the abuse and neglect he saw at-risk kids endure. For thirty-five years, Belisle "hung in there" because when you are a Mountie, and a Belisle, you never quit.

So, for thirty-five years, day in and day out, this master's-level clinical therapist persevered, just as he did when he was a senior playing on the very first Bill Belisle–coached Mount squad. After all, Coach Bill had prepared him to deal with life's challenges, hadn't he? When therapist John Belisle visited a school or a residence and was confronted by the images of cruelty inflicted upon the innocent, he tightened his chinstrap and emotional equipment and broke out a bongo drum or djembe or any other instrument he could use to help heal battered kids.

Then he went to work.

"Very few stay in the field [clinical therapy] that long, so I feel my ability to do that very much comes from Dad and his philosophy and work ethic," explains John Belisle. "My ability to hang in there and go to work every day

Forward Chris Murphy was a two-time all-star during the early 1990s. *Author's collection.*

and be around child abuse and some of the kids I work with, I think that's where some of my father's lessons were put into practice. I learned early on that you go out there, you give it your best, you don't complain, you suck it up and you go back out there and do it the next day. You don't quit—you never quit. I never heard my father talk about winning; when he was barking at you in the locker room, it was all about never giving up."

In a high-stress field where worker burnout is common, John Belisle persevered. For seventeen years, he worked for Casey Family Services, which provided case management for its parent company, the Annie E. Casey Foundation. The Casey Foundation had for thirty-six years provided "high-level foster care services to thousands of children and families through Casey Family Services." On December 31, 2012, it closed Casey Family Services in order to focus on a "grant-making strategy to improve outcomes for children and families." Belisle was one of approximately four hundred employees laid off.

But there was no way John Belisle was going to stop helping traumatized kids just because his job had been eliminated. In March 2013, he was back

# The Culture of Mount Saint Charles Hockey

Senior forward Pat Ciummo in action during the 2003 season. *Photo courtesy of Bill Belisle.*

at work—but now he was captain of his own team. "I am trying to start my own business that is semi-counseling oriented," he says. "Because I'm a percussionist, one thing I did in addition to counseling abused and neglected kids was to incorporate the music, and I always included drums and drum groups whenever I did therapy groups with kids. I utilized drums to help kids vent frustrations, express emotions and learn social skills and cooperation. I saw it grow over the years, so now I feel that I can make it business, whether as a residential program or in group homes, schools or different programs. Drum Groups Services is in the beginning stages. I hope to make a living from it. I'm confident that I can make it productive."

"What do you fear, Coach?"

It is a question likely not posed to Bill Belisle in recent interviews, if ever. Belisle, who is as quick with a command or a retort as a lion tamer is with a whip, pauses in thought. His eyes, usually sharp and sometimes as intense as a laser, vacillate repeatedly. Time passes—just seconds, but they seem a lifetime. Finally, Dave Belisle intercedes: "What does he fear? He's so fearless...I can't speak for him, but I would think what drives him, and why he's still doing this [coaching], is his fear that one day he won't be able to do this."

## A History of Mount Saint Charles Hockey

The Belisles experienced a measure of that fear when Coach Bill was sidelined for much of the 1983 campaign with a skull fracture. Today, he has only vague memories of the on-ice fall that nearly killed him. Dave Belisle, however, remembers the emotionally draining weeks and months that followed the near-tragic incident.

"It was a trying month," remembers Dave Belisle, who co-coached the Mounties with Tony Ciresi to the 1983 state title. Dave continues:

> *There were a few days when he was in a coma...I was scared about taking over the program. Thank God I had great players and a great assistant in Tony [Ciresi]. Then there was the fear of whether or not my father was ever going to be healthy again. I really feel for the Class of 1984. That was the team that handled the brunt of the Bill Belisle...trying to find himself. There were days when he'd scream at the kids and get angry, and there were days when he would cry. He couldn't control his emotions. It was worse on my mother because she was receiving the brunt of it. In our family, we were fearful he would never again be the person that he is: tough, confident, passionate—all those great things. We thought he would never come back. 1984 was very difficult; even winning that championship that year there was still doubt...he still wasn't the same. '84 was the most fearful time for all of us. You can see the* [get-well] *card...every kid in school signed it. I remember talking to LaSalle alumni; they, too, were saying prayers for Coach Bill Belisle. We weren't sure he was going to make it.*

There was a time, especially during the era of The Streak, when the media each autumn asked Bill Belisle how much longer he would coach at MSC. Belisle was prone to say he'd keep coaching as long as the Good Lord gave him the good health to continue. So far, he has. During practices and in games, Coach Bill still has complete command of his team, still finds ways to challenge his players with novel practice routines, still delights in winning state titles. He still runs what will soon be the new and improved Mount Saint Charles (née Brother Adelard) Arena. To even consider asking when Bill Belisle will retire is pure folly. This captain will go down with the Mount Saint Charles ship.

Dave Belisle, however, recognizes that both Rhode Island and Mount Saint Charles hockey are approaching a crossroads. Unless coaches from other New England parochial schools can find a way to create and support their own independent league, talented players will continue to follow the pipeline out of tradition-rich hockey programs, such as the Mount. At home, the patriarch of the Mount program, though healthy and in charge of "his house" on Logee Street, is approaching his mid-eighties and is in the sunset

# The Culture of Mount Saint Charles Hockey

*Above*: Three generations of Belisles (co-coaches Bill and Dave and 2013 captain Brian Belisle) accept the 2013 championship trophy after MSC swept LaSalle. *Photo courtesy of Ernest Brown.*

*Left*: Senior captain Brian Bailey looks to make a pass. *Photo courtesy of Bill Belisle.*

of his glorious career. Dave Belisle, meanwhile, is approaching his mid-fifties and has a successful business career and kids in college. Over the years, most Mount fans and mavens have assumed the younger Belisle would take over the program upon his father's retirement. Yet considering the "frustration" of battling against a stagnant economy, the dilution of player talent and the usual demands placed

*Above*: Right wing Brandon Castro had twenty-one goals and fifteen assists to lead Mount during the 2004–05 season. *Photo courtesy of Bill Belisle.*

*Right*: Luke McDonough was a first-line forward for the Mounties and one of the team's leading scorers during the 2003–04 season. *Photo courtesy of Bill Belisle.*

by parents, there's no guarantee Dave Belisle will run the Mount show when he approaches age sixty. For the moment, Dave Belisle is emotionally balancing between two worlds: today's, with Coach Bill at the helm and Mount savoring its forty-third state championship overall, and a future world without his beloved father and, perhaps, even himself running the program. "I don't even want to think of that," he said midway through the 2012–13 season. That's why, upon winning the 2012–13 title, son honored father as he has done time and again with an "I love you" and a gentle, respectful kiss on his dad's forehead. Every day that the Belisles are coaching and playing together is special.

Mount's Tyler Scroggins (#10) was an all-state selection in 2013 and the team's leading scorer. *Photo courtesy of Ernest Brown.*

Mount senior forward Daniel Glod (#16) passes to teammate Brian Belisle (#7), and the Mount captain seals Mount's forty-third state title with an open-net goal. *Photo courtesy of Ernest Brown.*

Captain Brian Belisle (left) and championship series MVP Daniel Glod (jumping) celebrate Glod's third-period goal in the Mounties' 2013 championship series–clinching victory over LaSalle Academy. *Photo Courtesy of Ernest Brown.*

"I always treat him as Coach," says Dave Belisle. "I know the effort that my kids put forth, but I also know the effort that he put forth, the sacrifices that we all made. This is all worth it."

No moment better captured the essence of Mount hockey than the postgame awards ceremony at Meehan Auditorium following Mount's state title victory in 2013. That's when three generations of Belisles accepted the championship plaque together. "My greatest moment was this year," says Dave Belisle, "when they finally said, 'Will the captain of Mount Saint Charles, Brian Belisle and Bill Belisle come and accept the award?' and we all went up together. My father turns and shows the trophy, and I got my hand on his shoulder, and my son has his hand on his other shoulder and turns and says, 'I love you, Pep [Pépère],' and I turn and say, 'I love you, Dad.' I've never had a better sports moment than that. There are so many memories, and we're all still here together—I never thought we'd be all together."

Then again, who thought MSC would win twenty-six straight titles or that Bill Belisle would become the most successful high school hockey coach in America? As long as Mount players, alumni and faculty further the spirit of the Brothers of the Sacred Heart and the academic and artistic curriculums of the academy, it's likely that no matter what coach blows the whistle at practice, Mount Saint Charles will always be a standard of hockey excellence by which other programs are measured.

# BIBLIOGRAPHY

### PERIODICALS

*Boston Globe*
*Hockey Digest*
*Hockey News*
*Hockey Night in Boston News*
*New Haven Register*
*Providence Journal*
*The Sporting News*
*Sports Illustrated*
*Woonsocket Call*

### BOOKS

Gillooly, John. *Pride on the Mount: More Than a Game.* Guilford, CT: The Lyons Press, 2005.
Mandeville, Charlie. *Mount Saint Charles Academy Hockey: How It All Started.* Self-published, 2010.

# Bibliography

## Websites

National Hockey League (www.nhl.com)
Rhode Island High School Hockey (www.rihsh.com)
Rhode Island Interscholastic League (www.riil.org)

## Interviews

Don Armstrong
Bill Belisle
Dave Belisle
John Belisle
Peter Belisle
Derek Chauvette
Tony Ciresi
Dave Duhamel
David Emma
Rob Gaudreau
Matt Grieve
Paul Guay
John Guevremont
John Harwood
Larry Kish
Dan Lavergne
Richard Lawrence
Ed Lee
Charlie Mandeville
Jeff Robison
Steve Shea
Garth Snow

# INDEX

## A

Adelard Arena  59, 85, 91, 107, 110, 119
American Hockey League  31, 72
Armstrong, Don  71, 91, 99, 100, 101, 102

## B

Belisle, Brian  15, 16, 138
Belisle, John  47, 52, 53, 61, 62, 131, 132
Belisle, Peter  127, 129, 131
Berard, Bryan  14, 73
Bishop Hendricken  71, 72, 87, 91, 99
Brother Adelard  19, 21, 22, 23
Brothers of the Sacred Heart  20, 21, 22, 57, 107, 114
Burrillville  24, 27, 28, 33, 34, 37, 38, 40, 41, 42, 45, 47
Burrillville High  24

## C

Capizzo, Peter  18
Chauvette, Derek  71, 127
Ciresi, Anthony, III  78
Ciresi, Tony  40, 78, 90, 92, 130

## D

Duhamel, Dave  92, 93, 101

## E

Emma, David  91, 99, 100, 103

## F

Flying Frenchmen  22, 23, 27, 29

## G

Gaudreau, Rob  71, 88, 89, 91, 99, 101
Guay, Paul  8, 14, 18, 69, 122
Guevremont, John  52, 109, 110, 112, 113, 114

## H

Harwood, John  32, 33, 37, 38, 40, 107

## L

LaSalle  36, 40, 65, 68, 85, 102, 116, 128, 134
Lavergne, Dan  72
Lawrence, Richard  19, 115, 116, 117
Lawton, Brian  14, 69, 113

# Index

Lee, Ed  119, 120, 121, 122, 123, 124, 125, 126
Lillibridge, Reynolds  32

## M

Mandeville, Charlie  30, 33, 34, 35, 38, 40, 102
Manocchia, Pat  68, 86
mills  20, 57
Mount Pride  18, 19, 24, 25, 30, 36, 40, 94, 107
Mousseau, Babe  37, 40

## N

New England titles  22, 27
1988 Mount-Hendricken  36
1983–84 season  69
1975–76 season  60
1974–75 season  51, 52, 53
1977–78 season  63
1972 championship  13
1972–73 season  47
1968–69 season  38, 39
1969–70 season  38
1967–68 state title  13

## P

Perry, Alan  69, 70, 103
Principals Committee on Athletics  39, 40
Providence College  30, 31, 71, 101

## R

Rhode Island Auditorium  23, 38, 41
Rhode Island Interscholastic League  21, 23, 123
Rhode Island Kings  46, 112
Robison, Jeff  71, 78, 87, 90, 93, 101
Russian style  51, 52, 53, 60

## S

Schneider, Mathieu  15, 71
Shea, Steve  48, 51, 53, 112

Snow, Garth  14, 71, 78, 91, 93, 100
Songin, Tom  39, 41
Summit Series  48, 51

## T

Tobin, Bernie  47, 48
Toll Gate  76, 77, 95
Tremblay, Larry  122

## W

Woonsocket  28
  mills  20

# ABOUT THE AUTHOR

Born and raised in Woonsocket, Rhode Island, Bryan Ethier grew up dreaming of playing goal for Mount Saint Charles but instead settled for covering the Mount Saint Charles hockey program for publications such as *Hockey Night in Boston News*, *The Sporting News* and *Hockey Digest*. He is the author of four nonfiction books and is a veteran columnist for the *Shore Line Times*.

*Visit us at*
www.historypress.net

This title is also available as an e-book

www.ingramcontent.com/pod-product-compliance
Lightning Source LLC
Chambersburg PA
CBHW042143160426
43201CB00022B/2390